MW01079278

Full Page Publishing

Essential Guide to Audio and Video Production

What you *really* need to know

2nd Edition

Robert G. Maier

FULL PAGE
PUBLISHING
New York - Oslo - Charlotte

Essential Guide to Audio and Video Production: What you really need to know 2nd Edition
Copyright © 2007, 2014 by Robert G. Maier
All rights reserved. No part of this publication may be reproduced, stored in a retrieval system, or transmitted in any form or by any means, electronic, mechanical, photocopying, recording, or otherwise, without the prior written permission of the publisher.

Full Page Publishing
411 Walnut Street
Davidson, NC 28036 USA
www.fullpagepublishing.com
(704)996-7724

Library of Congress Cataloging-in-Publication Data

Maier, Robert
Essential guide to audio and video production / by Robert Maier.
p. cm
1.
ISBN 978-0-9837708-7-9

10 9 8 7 6 5 4 3 2 1

SPECIAL THANKS TO:
Kate Carmody
Brian Scott
Kamran Mir Hazar
Ingrid Araya Russell

Contents

Introduction to this book 8

Section 1 **The Moving Image** 9

   Science and History of Moving Images/Motion Pictures 9

   Imaging Technical Basics 11

   Recording Video 17

Section 2 Camcorders 19

   Standard Video Camcorders 19

   DSLR Video Camcorders 19

   Camcorder Parts 20

   Camcorder Accessories 36

   Basic Camera Composition and Movement 46

Section 3 **Basic Lighting Techniques** 51

   Lighting Theory and Physics 51

   Lighting Equipment and Technology 53

   Safety/Comfort 59

   Three-point lighting 60

   Using natural light 61

   Chroma-key lighting 62

Section 4 **Video Editing** 63

   Editing Theory 63

   Sony Vegas Pro Video Editing Software Interface 67

   Components of Edited Programs 69

   Editing Work Flow 71

Section 5 Basic Audio for Video 78

   Microphones 78

   Other audio equipment 85

   Solving common recording problems 87

Audio in the TV Studio.. 89

Section 6   Directing Tips **91**

Shooting Process 91

    Basic Shooting Tips for the Videographer/Director 95

Running the Shoot.. 95

Studio Multi-camera Shooting 97

Section 7   Producing.. **98**

Proposals, Treatments, Scripts.. 98

Money management & budgeting... 100

Essential Video Terms 106

Video Production Work Flow.. 113

Section 8   Video Lists and Forms... **115**

Vegas Cheat Sheet 116

Field Shoot Checklist 117

Video Recording Service Request Form... 118

TV Commercial Production Checklist 120

Standard Audio/Visual Appearance Release.. 122

Production Office Supplies/Equipment 123

Sample Video Script 124

Call Sheet 125

Script Breakdown Sheet Sample 126

Sample Blank Production Budget.. 127

Tips for Clear Broadcast Writing.. 130

Sample Invoice   10101010 132

How to Get Your Name in the IMDb 133

Section 9 **Advanced Essentials of Audio Production** **134**

Characteristics of sound... 134

Music basics 135

Basic electronics for audio production... 136

Microphones 139

Digital Production 142

Mixing and Processing Audio... 145

Recorders/Media 149

Audio Chain/Studio Layout *150*

Music Recording Studio Basics *153*

Radio *155*

***Section 10* Audio Essential Lists** **156**

Protools Cheat Sheet *156*

Adobe Audition Hot Tips & Cheat Sheet *162*

Essential Audio Terms *163*

Jobs in the Field of Audio *172*

Tips for creating a recorded music playlist *174*

Common Radio Program Components *175*

Tips for Quality Radio/Audio Spot Production *176*

Recording Studio Preparation and Procedure Checklist *177*

Recording Studio Engineer Qualification Test *178*

Common Cable/Adapter/Connector Chart *179*

Introduction to this book

I have worked in media production for more than thirty years, taught in colleges, and held workshops. Individuals seeking a career in broadcasting, electronic journalism, audio and video production, sound reinforcement, require certain basic facts to ensure a good start. Hundreds of books on the subject are available, but I have found most to be over-written, inadequate, and overpriced for the digital world. This book is for beginners. It is what I cover in my college's Audio and Video classes.

A guide does not tell you everything about a subject. It points you in a direction and shows highlights of your learning journey. You should discover and explore details yourself. This is especially appropriate in the Internet age where access to up-to-date visuals, videos, articles, forums, and FAQs is so easy. Internet resources provide as much or as little detail as you want or need and are updated faster than any textbook. Use this book as a checklist to guide that search. Web links, are not provided in this book, because they change so quickly. Just search Google® for the latest and greatest.

Of course, some Internet information may have incorrect or unclear content. Check several links when confused. Each will likely have valuable information, and you will discover sources that are better for you than others. Keep track of them.

Don't limit your focus. I use this book for both Audio and Video classes because individuals with skills in both areas are much more likely to find work. The amount of Audio-Video specialist work far exceeds the number of radio or TV broadcasting jobs. Add to that a good dose of website creation/management, and you have excellent career possibilities.

Use the white space in this book for notes and reminders of items that are of interest to you. Audio and video production has tens of thousands of details, and no one can remember them all. Keep a paper or digital pad in your pocket or at your workstation to jot down occasional settings and procedures, you come across. You'll refer to it often, and save a lot of time.

Robert Maier

Section 1 The Moving Image

Science and History of Moving Images/Motion Pictures

Still Photos/Capturing Images

- **Camera Obscura**
    - o Used in Rome through the early 19th century
    - o Used by artists to cast image on paper or a wall, that could be traced and used as reference document.

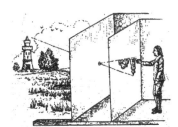

Camera Obscura from 16th Century

    - o In the 16th-17th centuries scientists discover when silver exposed to light, it darkens.
    - o 1827 - French inventors Niepece and Daguerre created first permanent photos using light-sensitive silver and chemical fixer; by 1840, photography was hugely popular

Motion Pictures

- o Theory of persistence of vision (flip books)
    - o Brain fills in gaps of quickly changing still images to create illusion of motion requires a still, black, still, black, sequence.
- o Minimum acceptable sustained illusion was tested to be 18 fps, modern is 24fps (movie theater) or 30fps video, because sound needed to travel at that speed to be intelligible.
- o Early pre-motion picture devices

- o British mathematician William George Horner invented the modern zoetrope in 1833. He called it the *Daedalum* (wheel of the devil). It did not become popular until the 1860s, when it was patented by makers in both England and America. The American developer, William F. Lincoln, named his toy the *zoetrope*, which means *wheel of life*.

Zoetrope

- o **Edweard Muybridge** made horse race photo sequences from line of still cameras and then flip books.
- o **Thomas Edison** invented the **kinetoscope**, a peep hole movie viewer (1st pay per view) in 1891 using 35mm motion picture film with sprocket holes.

Man peering into a kinetoscope about 1900

- o **The Lumiere Brothers** in France were the first to project motion pictures onto a screen.

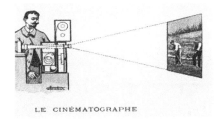

LE CINÉMATOGRAPHE

Imaging Technical Basics

The Frame

o A frame is made up of one still image taken from a sequence of images

- The sequence creates illusion of motion due to the principle of "**persistence of vision**"
- A frame is the smallest division of images in all motion picture/video processes; they cannot be divided
- Original motion picture frame was 35mm sprocketed film projected at 18 fps;
- In video, frames per second is variable, but generally frames per second (fps) is 29.97 fps, rounded to 30fps; modern HD video is 60 fps.
- There are many frame sizes; the most common in video production are:

Exposure

Over-exposed   Under-exposed   Normal exposure

- Exposure is the level of brightness of an image
  o Originally controlled mechanically by an "iris"
  o Now an electronic digital process
  o Images can be over-exposed, normal, or under-exposed
  o Exposure can be fixed to some extent in video editing programs but it is best to strive for normal.
  o It's easier to fix under-exposure than over-exposure, so it is generally better, to under-expose.
- Exposure is determined by several factors
  - Iris/Aperture – the opening in the camera where the lens connects to the camera body, light enters, and images are picked up by the
    o Older lenses mechanically adjust amount of light hitting CCD.
    o Newer cameras adjust aperture electronically by adjusting the sensitivity of CCD.
  - Shutter Speed
    o Adjusts length of time frame is exposed, and therefore the amount of light that hits the CCD—partially determining exposure level (brightness of image).
  - Focal Length of Lens

- o The higher the magnification (the more a lens is zoomed-in), the higher the light level is needed.
  - ▪ Gain Switch
    - • Electronically amplifies (increases) the light entering the video processor from the pickup chip.
    - • Gain can add grainy electronic noise, and should only be used when necessary; *generally better to increase brightness in post-production* where more precise controls are available.
  - ▪ ND Filters
    - • Neutral Density filters are optical quality glass or in some cameras, electronic settings that reduce the amount of light entering lens.
      - ▪ ND filters come in fixed measurements, usually noted as ND1, ND2, ND3, depending on the camera model.
      - ▪ In most digital cameras, ND filters are electronic switches, not physical glass filters.

Color

- ▪ Color is an element of the sense of sight that is differentiated by the various wavelengths of light reflecting into the eye.
  - • Color has three properties.
    - o Hue- the name of the color (red, yellow, blue, etc.)
    - o Intensity- the strength and vividness of the color. For example, we may describe the color blue as "royal" (bright, rich, vibrant) or "dull" (gray/blue).
    - o Value, meaning its lightness or darkness. Shade and tint refer to value changes in colors.

White Balance

The left photo has not been white balanced for outdoor light; the left photo has been white balanced (see color .pdf to view difference).

- White balance adjusts the camera so the dominant ambient light is set at white, ensuring correct presentation of color hues in recording and playback.
- Color Temperature: The hue radiated by a specific source of light, depending on the chemical composition of the source (eg. heated tungsten radiates a yellow hue). All items when heated will emit a different dominant color of the spectrum.
- Most light is dominated by a particular hue: daylight (blue); indoor tungsten (yellow); fluorescent (green)
- Other lights such as street lights, arena lights, security lights have other color temperatures, and dominant colors
- Adjusting the dominant hue to white will usually give a realistic color to all the other colors.

Contrast

Low Contrast   High Contrast

- Contrast is the difference between the darkest and the brightest parts of an image.
    - High contrast generally provides a sharper, clearer image.
    - Low contrast usually provides a foggy, muddy image.
    - Low contrast indicates under-exposure.

Focus

- Focus is the sharpness of the image and is adjusted on the camera by moving internal lens elements; sharp focus is critical for usable shots, except when seeking a special *soft focus* effect.

This image is out of focus.

- Depth of Field
  - Is the concept that a lens can only sharply focus on a small area in front of the lens. Focus is adjusted depending on the type of lens and the distance the subject is away from the camera. The actual depth of field is the amount of the depth in a shot that appears to be in focus. The depth of field can be wide or shallow.
  - The higher the iris setting (brighter the scene), the greater the depth of field.
  - The greater the magnification of a lens (the more zoomed-in), the smaller the depth of field.

  The second dancer is in the sharpest focus, showing a shallow depth of field. This was shot with the lens zoomed-in to achieve the shallow depth of field.

  - To adjust focus with a zoom lens, always zoom in to the subject, and then sharpen focus.
  - What looks in focus on small camera screen may look out of focus when seen 100 times larger on big screen
- Auto Focus
  - Most modern cameras have excellent auto-focus systems that are fast, smooth, and accurate. Auto focus should be used in the majority of situations.
  - **WARNING:** In HD cameras, focus may appear accurate on small camera screens, but when enlarged 100 or

more times on a large screen, focus errors are multiplied too. This is a good reason to use auto-focus, because the auto-focus mechanism is more accurate at judging focus than the human eye on a small screen.

o   Manual focus may be preferable when primary objects are deep in the frame, but objects close to the lens move through the frame and trigger auto focus, resulting in unwanted focus/de-focusing.

Recording Video

Time Code

Slate with time code

o   Time code is generated to give each frame a specific address; this enables editors to track and manage every video frame (store and playback).

- Time code is recorded in the video signal; it can be switched to be made visible or not; it can be set to a specific number or begin at zero.
- Time code has a range of 0-24 hours and is displayed for example as **12:24:55:28** (hours, minutes, seconds, frames)
- Free-run time code and non-drop time code should be selected.

Video and Audio Tracks

o   Video consists of a video (image) and at least one audio (sound) track; sometimes multiple audio tracks are recorded simultaneously with the video track. Camcorders generally record two audio tracks.

- Audio and Video tracks are recorded separately, but kept in sync because they have same time code addresses.
- Tracks are separated in the editing process.
- Using separate tracks provides greater editing flexibility.
- Multiple tracks of video and audio create richer visual and audio presentations.

File Types

o Audio and video are recorded in numerous digital file types.

o Each type has different **digital compression** formulas and sampling rates

o Common digital video file types are .avi, .mpeg2, .mpeg4, QuickTime (.mov) .wmv, avchd.

o File types accommodate various playback hardware, depending on the quality required of the playback image and sound.

o Larger file sizes enable higher quality image and sound. Some video files are shrunk (**compressed**) to play back on mobile phones; others are hardly squeezed in order to provide high resolutions needed for large screen projection; many are designed for on-line or partial computer screen viewing—as in YouTube videos.

o **Compression** controls parameters for screen size and audio quality.

o Files are initially recorded and edited in the highest quality file types. After editing, they are "rendered" to the file type and screen size required for the playback hardware and situation.

High Definition (HD) Video

o Old NTSC analog video had 525 lines of resolution.

o HD has 720 or 1080 lines of resolution.

o **i** is interlace scan; **p** is progressive scan, and highest quality

o HDMI connectors pass audio and video in high bandwidth also some data, including anti-copy protection.

o There are many **HD formats**, most camcorders feature only 2-3 Be sure your editing system handles the format you shoot in.

Section 2 Camcorders

Standard Video Camcorders

This is the common style of a traditional video camcorder, with the view screen open to see manual controls.

o   The standard video camcorder is based on traditional motion picture cameras which are designed with a long body.

o   The long body provides space for numerous manual controls like iris, steadi-shot, audio level, ND filters, white balance presets, zebra check, which are faster and easier to access than digging through internal menus that can be 3-4 levels deep.

DSLR Video Camcorders

DSLR (Digital Single Lens Reflex)camcorders look like traditional professional still cameras.They require accessories to function well as professional video tools.

o   The DSLR Camcorder is based on the traditional Single Lens Reflex still camera with a wide body.

o   DSLRs are growing in popularity for some good reasons.

- They allow a still photographer to use an existing expensive still photo lens collection which might include ultra-wide angle lenses and extreme telephoto lenses for video too.
- They allow the use of a single camera for both high-quality stills and video.

o However, DSLRs used traditional video shooting can be awkward to use because they require many add-on accessories.

DSLR Rig with mic, viewfinder, focus and zoom controls and more, can make an awkward, expensive shooting tool.

Camcorder Parts

The Lens

High-end Zeiss interchangeable zoom and prime lenses; the smaller are single focal length (prime) lenses.

- o The lens contains of several round glass elements that collect light and direct it to the camera's pick-up chip.
- o The housing includes a **focus ring** to adjust focus and a **zoom ring** to change the focal length (magnification).
- o Zoom Lens
    - The zoom lens provides many different focal lengths generally from 1:10 or 1:20 magnification strengths
    - The zoom allows continuous change of focal lengths in a shot to simulate camera movement, and create dynamic shots.
    - Most camcorders have built-in permanent zoom lenses.
        - Some high-end broadcast camcorders allow for interchangeable zoom lenses for special high magnification needs in sports or nature photography.
        - Most DSLR cameras accommodate "fixed focus/prime lenses" which are often higher quality or have specific "looks" favored by some directors of photography.
- Lens Accessories
    - o Polarizer to cut glare
    - o Lens tele-extender or wide angle adapters
    - o UV(ultra-violet) protects expensive lens from scratches
        - Lens cap- protects lens when camera not in use
        - Lens Shade (Shields from lens flares- light streaks seen in a lens pointed into a bright light source)

Prism

- Splits light into 3 primary colors and projects each color onto separate chip for better quality image capture

Video image pick-up chip

- Pro cameras have 3 chips, red, blue, green for each primary color
- Processing one color at a time results in higher quality
- Collects light, turns it into electrical pulses for conversion to digital signal
  - o   Pixels record color and brightness

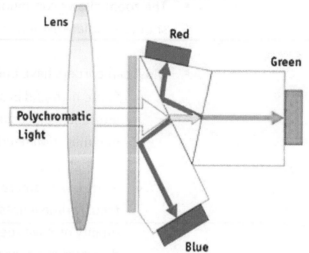

Three pickup chips record light split by prism, then are recombined electronically.

Camcorder Parts - Digital Section

Digital Converter

- Converts analog light to digital files via pixels embedded on a light pickup chip.

Digital Processor

- Adjusts various elements of light: color, hue, brightness, contrast, white balance, and black level in an image

Digital Video Recording Media

- Flash Memory Cards (SDHC)

SDHC flash memory cards have various capacities and can record several hours of HD video. 16GB is minimum for video, and records about 60 minutes.

  - o SDHC cards becoming most popular camcorder format
    - Erasable, light weight, fast transfer to computer, small size,
    - Real-time capture process not required
    - More durable than video tape
    - Larger video capacity than any tape format
    - Low comparative cost per recorded minute
- Hard drives
  - o Internal to camera
    - More compact size
    - Storage limited
    - Require camera when downloading
  - o External
    - Larger storage capacity (250 gB+)
    - Do not tie up camera for downloading
    - Expensive
    - Mostly for professional use

- Video Tape- Analog and Digital

The Mini-DV cassette (1/4" tape), still used occasionally, is the last type of professional videocassette that began with the ¾" Sony U-matic format which deputed in the early 1970s and enabled much lower-cost video production.

- o More than 12 video tape cassette formats are/were used professionally to record analog and digital **NTSC** video. NTSC is a low resolution, no longer broadcast in the US, but works for some on-line use.
  - Mini-DV was the last prosumer tape cassette format developed for recording HD, but has been mostly replaced by SDHC and other Digital Memory Cards.
  - Analog video recording is a legacy format, including two-inch, one-inch, three-quarter inch and half-inch tapes (**Betacam** format) that many producers have in their archives, but rarely use to produce—at least in the U.S.A.
- o HDCAM, DVCAM, and DVCProHD are still major HD digital video tape formats, and millions of cassettes in those formats remain in tape libraries.
  - Many TV stations still use HDCam or HDV tape camcorders/cassettes for day-to-day news operations because they may have many expensive field cameras in that format, and do not want to spend hundreds of thousands of dollars on new gear that provide the same image quality as tape-based camcorders.

Camcorder Parts-Other

Audio

- Mic
  - o Internal
    - Doesn't have effective windscreen
    - Only for wild sound or very close-up shots
  - o External-camera mounted mics

    Camcorder with external microphone
    - Have effective windscreen and shock mount capabilities
    - Can use for wild sound and better quality
  - o Better to use external non-camera mounted mic on boom or stand, hand-held or lavaliere
  - o Best professional practice is not to see mic in shot— sometimes difficult to achieve in a-
    - High noise situation
    - Fast-moving, unpredictable situation
  - Mic controls
    - o Phantom Power- supplies condenser type mic with 48volt electric power supply
      - Should not be used with mic that has internal mic battery, or non-condenser mic
    - o Att. (attenuator)
      - Reduces audio sensitivity in very loud situations (race tracks, loud factories, air strips)
      - Rarely needed

- o Line/mic select-
  - ▪ Line; for high-level line audio from external mixer or other amplified sound source
  - ▪ Mic; for any directly connected mic—lower power; pre-amp in camera amplifies to line level
- o Audio input level controls

  - ▪ Adjust amount of loudness input, usually with rotating wheel
  - ▪ Usually a wheel or knob on the camcorder
  - ▪ Used for mic or line level
- o Audio Level Meter

  Typical 2-channel digital audio level meter
  - ▪ A digital readout on the viewfinder using a scale to show the incoming volume level
  - ▪ In color meters
    - o Green marks mean audio is undistorted;
    - o Yellow marks mean audio is approaching maximum
    - o Red marks mean audio has exceeded peak level and will be distorted
  - ▪ If audio quality is critical, and if audio is continually in red area, stop recording, re-adjust audio downward and re-shoot.
- ▪ Channel Output Select
  - • Most video has two accompanying audio channels embedded with the video
  - • Selects Ch1 or Ch2 or both per input to send signal to different audio tracks for independent control of audio signals (e.g. 2 person interview where each has an individual mic)

- Headphone/Speaker monitor volume level
    o Audio must be listened to while recording so extraneous noise and distortion will not be recorded; use headphones to be sure audio is working; do not depend only on level meter.
    o Internal loudspeaker in most cameras is weak and low quality, and should not be used.
    o Headphone speaker generally low, best to use extra sensitive headphone—cheap ear buds can be best.
        - Automatic audio level or gain controllers (AGC) should only be used in emergencies because their accuracy is poor.

- Audio inputs

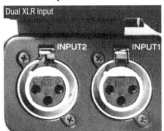

All professional camcorders have 2 internal XLR audio inputs.

    o XLR connection is most professional, because highest quality; can be used for mic or line level inputs
    o Mini-phone connector (1/8 inch) is only audio input is found on mostlower end camcorders and DSLR cameras
- for higher quality and more versatility, an external mixer with XLR inputs and a mini-phone output are available

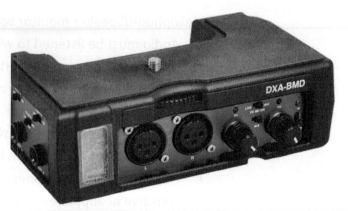

This external mic pre-amp/mixer attaches beneath a camcorder or DSLR camera with a screw.

Battery

A typical camcorder battery measures about 1.5"x3"

- The bigger and heavier the battery, longer it powers and the more expensive it is.
- External 12v power adapters are available to plug into wall sockets of car electric outlets, and replace batteries, which generally will operate a camcorder for less than 2 hours.

Common Manual controls

- Manual is preferred over auto in professional situations
  - o Creates more consistent results
  - o Automatic changes usually too slow to react and distract
- o Lens controls
  - ▪ Focus/Autofocus mode
    - Autofocus is faster; it's more precise than manual, and results in sharper focus because of low-rez viewfinder
    - Zoom/Focus/Iris Ring

- Manual adjustment ring on the lens controls a choice of 3 functions ring on the lens
  - Zoom Ring Control Switch

This switch on the side of the camera selects the zoom ring function in the front of the lens.

  - Zoom servo/manual switch

    - The zoom ring can be operated manually or by the servo motor according to the setting on this switch. **Moving the zoom ring manually, when this switch is in servo, may damage the servo motor.**

      o Zoom Speed

        - Zoom speed control changes from slow (1) medium (2) fast (3)
        - 2 places to control- top handle handgrip
    - Iris
      - The iris controls the amount of light reaching the pick-up chip. It is like a window. The smaller the window, the less light can enter.
      - Auto Iris or auto exposure causes problems
        - Exposure changes suddenly reacting to objects of different brightness moving through frame, which is amateur-looking.

- Momentary Auto Exposure Button
  - Use for quick exposure setting, then reverts to manual control, so you get the benefit of auto exposure without the problem.
  - Be sure the camera does not remain on auto exposure setting
- Shutter speed
  - Controls amount of time frame is exposed, measured in small fractions of a second (1/60 slowest usable without smear)
  - While the iris is an adjustable hole that is always open, the shutter is a gate that is either open or closed. The longer time the shutter is open, the larger amount of light hits the pickup chip.
  - The shutter is an important element in the **persistence of vision** concept which requires a moment of black so that a frame can change without smearing.
- **ND Filter**
  - Reduces chip sensitivity in bright light situations (beach, snow)
  - 2 levels of darkening and off
- Processing switches

Some cameras nest processing switches

- White balance (**see page 12 for image**)
  - o Adjusts camera so that white is the basis for all color despite oddly colored light in scene; works well where small color shift occurs, but in strongly colored will not.
- Zebra button
  - o Zebra lines displayed over the viewfinder image warn of imminent over-exposure.

Zebra lines show over-exposed areas.

- Steadishot (EIS or other name)
  - o Electronically and/or optically reduces shaky hand held camera movement.
  - o Software in post can accomplish same effect, maybe better
  - o Picture Profile/Scene select/etc.
    - ▪ Adds pre-set and/or user-selected color/brightness effects.
    - ▪ Better done in post-production

Miscellaneous camera body manual controls

These common manual controls are found on a camcorder body; some units use different terms, some cameras do not have all these controls.

- Status check
  - o displays various combinations of camera menu settings or activities in view finder

- o Sometimes called "Display" or both buttons included on some cameras
- Battery release
  - o Releases battery lock so battery can be removed
- Flash memory card bay
  - o Insertion point for SD or similar cards, usually covered with small door
- Still photo button
  - o Activates digital still photo feature found in many camcorders
- Focus Boost
  - o Magnifies for low-light situations, critical focus on small details in distance
- ASSIGN buttons
  - o Programmable for quick switching to pre-set setting
  - o Menu button and selector switches
    To activate internal menu and scroll through choices
  - o Push button to select item

- Auto-lock/Hold
  - o Prevents accidental activation of manual button while handling camera (good idea!)
- Gain
  - o Electronic amplification of light for very low light
  - o Not recommended because adds noise.
  - o Excusable as an effect, or emergency situation
  - o Usually 1st level is not bad and good in normal low-light interior or early evening or shots in shadow.

Miscellaneous internal digital menu controller

All camcorders have external panels to control internal menu choices, above is a common configuration.
- Cameras have varying options and names
- Up to 100 main choices; sometimes 5-6 sub menu choices and adjustments; that's over 500 different settings
- Many choices are not regularly used
- Most operators do not have all menu choices memorized
  - Always have owner's manual handy as reference tool
- When camera has multiple users, it pays to run through the common settings to be sure camera is set to your choices.

Recorder Switches
- Camera On/Off

This switch usually has a lock mechanism that requires an extra step so unintentional power-off, which would ruin a recording, is avoided. It can include a record on/off switch.
- Record on/off switches
  - Usually in 2-3 places on camera
    - Uses a thumb switch
    - On camera top handle
    - Sometimes on front under lens on more high-end camcorders
    - Also found on handgrip

- Playback switch
    - o Uses common playback direction/speed/pause switches
    - o Usually located on side of camera under swing-out viewfinder

Viewing-Monitoring

- LCD Panel Viewfinder

Camcorder with LCD Panel Viewfinder open with Eyepiece viewfinder at rear.

- ▪ The LCD panel viewfinder is not good in bright light situations, because images can get washed out; it is not a good judge of focus; use for image composition, or viewing playback.
    - Use also to view internal control menus.
- ▪ The screen can swivel on 2 axis for easier viewing.
- ▪ Mirror option for self-shooting by rotating 180 degrees on vertical axis.
- ▪ High power consumption- do not use if battery power is low.
- ▪ Internal menu for image adjustment of brightness, contrast, saturation, etc.
- Eyepiece Viewfinder (see above image)
    - ▪ Best used for fine focus adjustment
    - ▪ Better viewer for bright light
    - ▪ Sometimes its brightness etc. adjusts via internal menu

Other Connections

- DC External Power Input
  - Sometimes will charge camera while operating- check specs
- HDMI- Handles HD video including audio
  - Prosumer or consumer primarily.
  - 20 ft. max cable run before image deteriorates.
- SDI – serial digital interface; a high-end digital signal used only in professional camcorders; transmits audio, video, timecode.
  - Uses BNC connectors and coax cable
  - Can run hundreds of feet without deterioration, so best suited for studio use.
- Monitor video only out
  - For external monitor—client, focus check, or large screen composition comparison
    - Can be RCA if analog video or BNC for digital
    - No audio on this output, except if HDMI

Camcorder Accessories

Operator's Manual

This is essential when shooting in field to check unfamiliar settings and camera or trouble-shooting.

External mic mixer

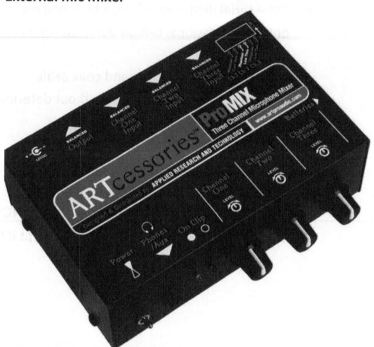

This small battery-operated mixer is allows adjusting and recording up to 4 mics at one time.

- Connects additional microphones to camera
- Blends several audio sources (mic or line) into one audio channel of the camera, with independent volume and frequency control for each source.
- Allows adjusting audio without jostling the camera
- Generally operated by **"sound recordist"** working with videographer

Tripod

- Three-legged support stand for camera that can be adjusted for height; it holds the pan head

Pan head

- Used to pan or tilt camera by hand using a handle
- Quality pan heads use fluid damping (like a shock absorber) to smooth movement
- Cheaper pan heads use friction brakes, and sometimes springs that grab and jump and usually give poor quality movement.
- Pan is left-right movement; Tilt is up-down movement
- Professional pan heads include a circular bubble level to aid in adjusting level

The green spot on the tripod head is the bubble level. It has an LED lamp to view at night or in dark studio spaces.

Camera base plate

- Attaches camera to tripod pan head to enable quick release when moving camera for handheld shooting or moving to a new set-up
- This small piece is critical and is easily misplaced or forgotten
- Many people leave the base plate on the camera, but it is actually a part of the tripod, because all baseplates are made for only one tripod pan head

Lens accessories

- Effects Filters
  - Polarizers are made of tinted glass and screw on to the front of a lens to cut glare from glass, water, or the sky, to create sharper, clearer images.

- Color Filter- Some glass filters can subtly change colors, but they are increasingly being replaced by digital processing.
- Star Filter- a glass filter that is finely etched to create "stars" in the image (see below).

Practical Lens accessories

o Wide-angle adapter- expands field of view beyond normal

o Telescopic adapter- magnifies the image

o UV filter/protector – cuts UV rays, but more importantly protects sensitive front lens element from scratches, splashes, thumbprints, and dirt.

- Lens shade- blocks direct shafts of bright light from entering the lens and creating unwanted **lens flares** (circles or bubbles of very bright light that obstruct the primary image)

Lens cap- tightly covers lens and protects from dirt and scratches, also prolonged exposure to bright light that can damage the pickup chip. Used when storing the camera.

Rain shield

- A tight-fitting shield that keeps a camera dry in wet situations, and allows use and access to view and operate camera controls.

Camcorder wrapped in rain shield

Carrying Case

Kata makes a wide variety of professional cases.

- Camera cases are durable, water, dust resistant and padded cases that protect the camera when it is not in use.
- Has pockets and space for carrying accessories like batteries, charger, cables, mic, headphones, manual, and media.

Slate- for multi-camera shooting

- Provides a simultaneous visual and audio reference point for syncing multiple cameras **(see "Timecode").**

Misc. support options

- Steadicam/Glidecam – balanced hand-held support that steadies hand-held movement using inertia

Glidecams, Steadicams, and other camera stabilizers come in many sizes and cost from $200 to $45,000.

- Steadibag- a light beanbag that makes an flexible surface that will allow leveling a camera on surfaces that cannot easily accommodate a tripod (car hood, rock, table)
- Lowboy- a camera mount that sits a few inches from the floor to allow extreme low-angle shots.
- Car mount- attaches camera to car exterior (hood/door) for moving shots.

Teleprompter

This teleprompter is mounted on a tripod. The camera is mounted behind the prompter screen.

- Camera mounted device that allows projection of text fed from a computer onto a glass screen in front of the lens so talent can read scripts while looking directly into camera.
- The camera can move, and the talent can still read by following the prompter, providing a natural, flowing performance. Camera external monitor

External video monitor mounted on a DSLR camera. The swivel mount adjusts viewing angles to allow several observers beside the camera operator.

- Used so others besides camera operator can view live shot or playback; or camera operator has more flexible viewing options.
- External monitors require battery or AC/DC adapters.

- They can be critical for judging focus, exposure, and color quality.

On-camera light

- Small light mounted just above lens to light faces of interviewees, usually used in news shooting
- Not an attractive light, but practical in certain low-light situations
- The above light is a cool, bright, lightweight LED.
- Light is powered by internal batteries or external AC/DC adapter

Camcorder Care

This kit can be bought for a few dollars and can make a big difference in the quality of your images.

- Lenses can collect dirt and dust that degrade your images.

- Lenses have very fragile coatings that can be easily scratched. Ideally, use a brush/air bulb cleaner to brush away dust.
- Avoid touching the lens with anything by putting a clear UV filter on the front of the lens. They are cheap and may be cleaned with anything. If they get scratched, throw them away and get a new one.
- Clean very lightly with soft lens cleaning cloth or specially manufactured lens cleaning tissue
- Use special lens cleaning fluid with a light touch.

Temperature

- Hi ambient heat can hurt electronics and lens
- Very cold can make electric motors and gears run slowly
- Going from cold to hot causes condensation to form on the lens.
- Never leave a camera in vehicle in the sun where temperatures can reach 140 degrees+
- Use a shade or umbrella when shooting for long periods in hot, direct sun

Shock protection

- Do not leave camera where it might fall
- Store camera in case when it isn't in use.
- Secure the case so it won't fall
- **NEVER** leave a camera unattended on tripod
- Lock tripod legs and tripod head

Theft

- Never leave camera in an unlocked, unattended room or vehicle, or where it can be seen by a casual observer
- When pausing on a shoot, store camera only in locked trunk of a car (consider temperature), otherwise carry it with you.

Dirt, dust, and moisture avoidance

- Dirt and dust can damage all moving parts in a camera—avoid them.

- Clean exterior with soft slightly moist cloth when dusty
- Do not expose the camera in dusty places or set it on a dirty/dusty surface
- Do not let camera get wet. Dry immediately if accidentally gets rain on it.
- Carry a plastic bag to protect camera in case of unexpected rain or dusty conditions
- Shoot under an umbrella if you must be in the rain.
- Be extremely careful when shooting in a boat. Do not let the camera out of your hands.

SDHC Chips

- Label memory chips with name and number before putting into camera
- Check chip capacity; format chips in camera if necessary
- Formatting chips erases all existing content on the chip
- Enable record-protect switch *after* chip is removed
- Bring back-up chips
- Put chips in a small "chip case" to protect and keep track of them.

8 Must-do Checks

> ## 8 MUST-DO Checks <u>Before</u> Shooting Video
>
> 1. Set all camera controls to manual
> 2. Set focus on the subject of the shot
> 3. Set shutter speed
> 4. Set iris/exposure on subject of the shot
> 5. Set zebra to 95%
> 6. Set white balance
> 7. Set proper video format (1080 or 720 etc.)
> 8. Level the tripod head

Basic Camera Composition and Movement

Composition and balance

o   Keep a pictorial balance in the frame. Every object in the frame should have an equally attractive—not necessarily identical-- element to keep the balance. Balance means when looking at the image it does not look like it will tip over.

This portrait c. 1490 is an example of the standard for portrait composition developed by Renaissance artists and still exists today. Modern TV directors insist on the same composition more than 500 years later.

This screen shot illustrates shows good standard video composition. When two persons are on camera, top of head, eyes, and shoulders should be on the same horizontal line.

Guide to good composition

o **Rule of Thirds** divides a frame into 9 equal rectangles; edges of objects in the frame should match a column edge; brightness, and color should be placed around frame so they balance.
- Eyes should align with the bottom of the first third.
- Diagonals represent action and movement

o Converging parallel lines create depth through perspective

o Shots from low angle make subjects look powerful, domineering

o Shots from high angle make subject look weaker,

o Include well-known objects in shots to show scale

o Blank/negative space can make a powerful image; don't stuff the frame full of objects; blank space in a frame calls more attention to the primary subject

o It is frequently nice to be slightly off from perfect balance.

o **All visual persons in broadcasting should study basic graphic design to be familiar with how good composition is achieved.**

Vertical headroom

- Headroom is a comfortable amount of space between the top of a person's head and the top of the frame.
- Headroom can refer to the human head or any principal object in the frame: glass of beer, dog, car, etc.

"Leading" in frame composition

o   People in interviews should be "led" by the camera operator; with more empty space in the direction they are looking.

This person is being interviewed by someone camera right, so more space is included frame right to make the space feel less cramped.

Creating depth

Foreground objects: include foreground objects to create depth of field. Pump is in focus, trees on the right are not.

Leading lines: diagonals and converging parallel lines lead to a single point to create depth and a dynamic composition.

Camera movement

- o Perform camera moves smoothly and slowly to avoid **strobe artifacts** and achieve better control.
- o **Feather** all moves (feather means to start up slowly and slow down slowly- don't jerk your starts and stops)
- o Allow **lead room** (space in the direction of movement) when following a person or moving object.

- o Rehearse moving shots or do multiple takes
- o Focus every shot first— When using manual focus, zoom in to subject; focus and rack back and forth while rolling to prove focus to editor; then shoot
- o Check the tripod's bubble level to be sure camera is level
- o Loosen **pan head locks** for smoothest moves.

Options for the editing room

o   Allow 2 -3 seconds hold still at head and tail to allow for dissolves and other transitions

o   Make shots about 5 second duration

o   Add moves to still shots so editors have a choice; include a combination of slow creep-in, creep-out, tilt up, tilt down, pan left-right, add an unusual angle

Safe areas

Safe areas view in Sony Vegas preview window

- Safe area lines are superimposed on the edges of the viewfinder frame where information can be lost due to screen cut-offs.

Exposure Tips

- Exterior
  - If sun is too harsh or bright, shoot in shady spot; partly cloudy/hazy skylight is best
  - In bright sun, sun should shine on your subject.
  - When shooting in the shade, avoid bright areas in the frame that will be over-exposed (**washout**).
- Interior
  - Avoid bright walls as backgrounds.
  - Avoid busy backgrounds.
  - Avoid bright windows or other bright spots in your frame.
  - Soften lighting by using indirect or diffused light.

Section 3   Basic Lighting Techniques

Lighting Theory and Physics

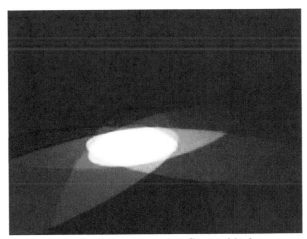

- Incidental and reflected light
  - Incidental is strong from one direction; creates shadows
  - Reflected is light and diffuse, coming from numerous directions and doesn't create sharp shadows
- Goals for lighting
  - Adequate exposure
  - Realism
  - Communicate emotion
- Sensitivity of human eye vs. video camera
  - Eye has contrast ratio of 100:1
  - Video cameras are about 30:1
  - Lighting must help overcome this differential, reducing contrast ratios by lighting areas that are not seen clearly due to high contrast ratios
- Color Temperature
  - All light has different temperatures depending upon:
    - Nature of source (sun, tungsten, HMI, mercury, LED,); when heated or charged with electricity, different elements glow with emphasis on different colors

- Tungsten is 3200k
- Daylight is 5200k
- Fluorescent tends green
  - o Filters and ambient light conditions influence color
    - Examples: Clouds in sky, smog in sky, room color, tinted windows, reflection from nearby objects.
- Shaping and adding texture with light
  - o Shadows
    - Help create 3 dimensionality in 2 dimensional images
    - define details
    - flat light is difficult to perceive
  - o Mood
    - Besides establishing basic rules of good composition, Renaissance artists experimented with high and low key lighting techniques
    - Low Key Lighting—can be plain and boring
      - Bright overall illumination; low contrast

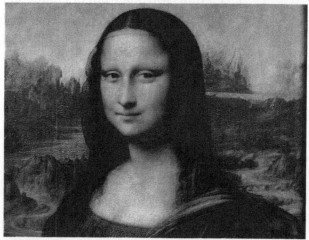

This classic portrait uses even, *low-key lighting*.

- High Key Lighting—dramatic, lively, dynamic
  - Selective areas are lit; high contrast

This painting uses uneven, *high-key lighting.*

- Varying Degrees and combinations of high and low are best

Lighting Equipment and Technology

This portable lighting kit from Lowell includes lights, stands, gels, electric cords, light flags and other equipment, including a case to carry it all.

Lighting sources

- o Tungsten/Quartz/Halogen bulbs
  - Hi-wattage, high temperature bulbs

- Warm yellowish color temperature, controllable because single strong source

Tungsten bulbs are small, but use a lot of energy and get hot enough to injure skin.

- Fluorescent bulbs
  - Cool, flat diffuse source, fragile
  - CFL units growing in popularity, used as multiple screw bases to make large flat diffusion
  - Some long tube units are large and bulky, though not heavy
  - Use less electricity

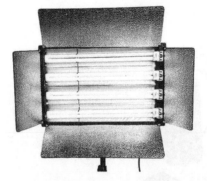

Flourescent lights are cool running but are large and the bulbs are expensive and fragile, and not useful as spotlights.

- LED
  - Cool to touch, small multiple small sources make it diffuse, light, not fragile, low power requirements

- Hi-tech instruments now focusable, and multiple standard color temperatures and can emit a wide range of colors, so colored gels not necessary.

This small LED unit emits a lot of light, is durable, lightweight, runs cool, and runs a long time off a battery. LEDs are being developed as focusable spotlights and soft lights.

- HMI
  - Very bright and large- daylight only, require heavy ballast, require less electricity
  - Expensive and heavy- mainly used by feature films needing lots of light

nStyles of Lights

Modern LED 4"Fresnel focusable spotlight

- Focusable
- Non-focusable
- Lens
- Open-face

- Softlight

Modern LED Soft Light Panel with diffusion panel over LED bulbs
  - No Lens- not focusable
  - Soft, smooth even light
  - Create softer shadows than spots
- Mounting hardware for lighting instruments
  - Hanging mounts
  - Floor Stands
  - Clamps
- Most essential accessories/grip equipment
  (due to space limitations, we do not include photos of all light and grip equipment. Visit Matthews Studio Equipment's website to view the hundreds of items listed in their lighting accessories and grip equipment catalog **http://www.msegrip.com/product.html)**

  - Sandbags- for weighing bottom of light stands to keep them from tipping
  - Extension cords
  - Safety ropes and cords
  - Gaffers tape
  - Apple boxes/wedges
  - C-stands
  - Tool kit
  - Leather gloves- protect hands from hot instruments

- Lighting control devices
  - **Barn Doors**

    Barn doors are mechanical shutters that control horizontal and vertical spill from lighting instruments.

  - **Diffusion**- translucent material that softens light
  - **Black Wrap**- aluminum foil painted black to guide or cut sections of light
  - **Black Cards**- black sheets of stiff card stock paper to guide or cut sections of light
  - Black fabric for large windows- used to eliminate unwanted window light spill
  - **Flags/spots/cutters**- fabric wrapped frames that can be mounted on light stands to guide or cut sections of light

    Flag mounted on a "C-stand"

  - **Dimmers**- Dimmers control the amount of brightness of a lighting instrument through electro/mechanical resistance.
  - **Bounce cards** or surfaces (ceilings, walls)- White sheets of stiff card stock paper used to bounce diffuse light onto a subject

○ **Reflectors** are shiny boards or discs that are generally used outdoors to reflect sunlight onto subjects, in place of powered lighting instruments.

This is a 4ft. diameter light weight disc reflector. Its multiple layers can reflect a warm light, be used as a diffuser, or be covered in black to be used as a cutter.

○ **Cookie—Cucoloris** – casts broken shadows on a background to provide interesting, abstract but not distracting shadows, like sunlight through trees.

This cucoloris breaks up light to create indistinct shadows on the wall to create texture and dimension.

Safety/Comfort

- Light bulbs and housings can be hot enough to burn flesh
  - Use gloves
  - Use pliers or other grippers to adjust hot barn doors
- Video equipment uses potentially fatal amounts of electricity
  - Think twice before handling electric cables
  - Always work with a helper
  - Turn off mains, when possible
- Wear leather gloves when handling hot tungsten lights; they can burn skin off in a second.
- Do not overload electrical circuits
- Know where the shooting room's circuit breakers are, in case you blow a breaker.
- Do not use frayed electric extension cords
- Instruments can be heavy and have sharp edges, fall and hit people
  - Use safety cords when hanging a lamp from a grid or wall
  - When light is on a stand, use sandbags on the bottom as counterweight to steady the load
- Power cords can trip people
  - Tape them down or cover them with runners where a lot of foot traffic
  - Warn visitors and greenhorns to be careful of cables
- Bright lights can damage vision/give sunburn
  - Don't stare into them
  - Can distract/irritate talent
    - Change lighting so it's not so harsh
    - Work as quickly as possible
- Sometimes lights must be hung high and require ladders and reaching in unbalanced positions
  - Have a helper always hold a ladder
- Never pack hot lights in cases
  - They can melt the plastic in the case

o   Lights can require 5-10 minutes to cool to handling temperature

Three-point lighting

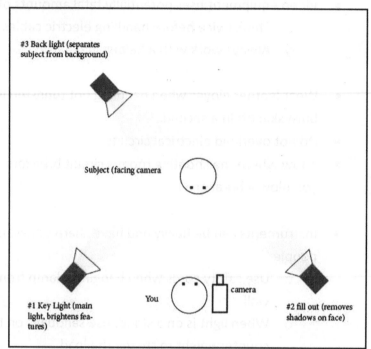

This example of 3-point lighting shows the backlight at an angle. Individual taste governs exact placement of the backlight.

- **Key light** – the main, strongest light source; can cause unwanted shadows
- **Fill light**- a softer light meant to fill in shadows or balance contrast
- **Back light**- a light in back of the subject that puts light on the top of the subject, creating a "rim light" glow that separates the subject from its background and creates an illusion of depth in the frame.
- **Lighting Ratio**- Key should be about 50% brighter than fill
- 3-point lighting can be difficult in multi-subject situations because it creates multiple shadows.

- Shadows
    - Are usually a problem and should be avoided
    - Additional lighting units to fight shadows
    - Close backgrounds a problem (e.g. Writing on a white board)
    - Lighting angles can be adjusted to reduce problem; the higher the light angle, the lower the shadow is projected
    - Flat/soft lighting is only solution to completely eliminate shadows
    - Camera composition can help reduce shadows
    - Sometimes impossible to remove all shadow problems because people move and lights don't

Using natural light

This stunning, natural-looking portrait was lit only with sunlight entering through a window.

- Natural light enters through windows or "practical" lighting instruments (practical: naturally occurring lighting instruments like table lamps)
    - Natural light can substitute for a key or fill, if color temperature matches instruments.

    - Normal bright sunlight can be too harsh
        - Must be filtered with diffusion of some sort

- Must be filled in with reflector or daylight balanced spotlight
  o Requires choosing a spot with existing indirect light
    - If existing indirect light is good just one light may be enough
  o Can save a lot of time
  o Sometimes 3 point lighting can look very artificial "TV-designed" and take away spontaneous look—depends on the design scheme
  o Always face subject into the sun so face receives maximum light (except for special efx)

Chroma-key lighting

Chroma Key or Green Screen is a common effect that changes a background through an electronic process.

- Requires a specific, narrow band of a bright color, which is electronically replaced by an image in a video switcher or editor with chroma-key capability.
- Chroma-key Green is the best color; but blue is very common
- Requires overall even brightness
- Used in everything from action movie spectaculars to local TV weather reports.
- Allows very inexpensive virtual digital backgrounds to replace actual physical sets, which can also make studio production move much more quickly.

Section 4 Video Editing

Editing Theory

- History

Moviola **film editing machine. Invented in the 1920s it allowed editors to play, rewind, and cut movie film frame by frame for precise arrangement of scenes. They ceased manufacture in the 1970s as video production and editing became superior technology.**

- The first motion pictures were never edited.
- Early directors discovered that bad shots could be cut out and story constructed using good shots only.
- They discovered that time and place and story pacing could be re-arranged with editing.
- They discovered that viewing experience could be enhanced by editing.
    - Complex stories could be told with edited motion pictures
    - Editing enables time to compress and the story to progress at a speed different from real time through "cut-aways."
  - **Cut-aways** are like a magic trick: they distract viewer while main scene changes time, characters, and/or location.

Editing Structure
- All motion pictures (video) are divided into individual images (frames) that are recorded in a consecutive sequence as they occur in real time measured in **frames per second.**
  - Editing has always consisted of a database of media. Portions of the media are assembled in a specific sequence that flows in a time line to tell the story.
- Digital editing
  - In film and tape editing, when a cut was made, it was a physical cut on the original media, making it very difficult to re-construct the change the edit point, which restricted choices.
  - Digital editing is "**non-destructive.**" Original material is never cut, and immediately available to try other editing possibilities.
  - Digital editing creates a list of where cuts occur, and what portion of the digital media is used.
  - The instructions of where the media is placed is called an **edit decision list.**
  - Multiple tracks of audio, video, and data can easily be played simultaneously, and changed individually

Language of editing
- Editing has certain processes that communicate specific ideas
- **Cut**
  - Changes scene, time, place, or character for story progression
  - Cuts can be nearly invisible in the story flow, or they can be shocking.
  - Cuts generally assume that no time passes between the cuts, but not always.
- **Transition**
  - Transitions (like **dissolves**) generally indicate a some passage of time, a substantial location change, or a substantial shift in the storyline.

A dissolve fades out one image while another fades in. It is an unnatural effect created by early filmmakers to smooth the change of time or place. Early movie-goers were sometimes confused by dissolves and had to learn the "film vocabulary" that transitions communicated major changes of time and place.

- Transitions can be over-used with fancy kitschy "preset" designs that look amateur.

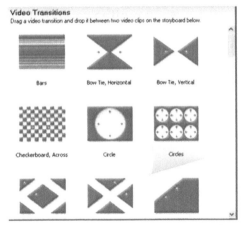

A selection of transitions in Windows Movie Maker and most editing programs. Most are overused-avoid them.

- Pace in editing
  - The faster the pace, the more energy is created for frantic mood, but can be tiring and confusing if used too much.
  - A slow pace creates romantic, thoughtful, relaxed mood, but can be boring if used too much.

- How to proceed with the editing process
  - Editing is choosing a logical sequence, by controlling the length and pacing of shots to tell a story.
  - The director collects the shots
  - Must deliver a sufficient variety of shots to tell the story in an interesting, accurate manner.
  - Typical shots include
    - Master (wide)
    - Facial Close-ups
    - 2-shots (2 people talking)
    - Over the shoulder close-up
    - Variety of cutaways of "B" roll as safety "go-to" shots or critical plot/action elements
  - Director's primary purpose is to get an interesting and clear collection of shots
  - The editor chooses the correct timing and pacing during editing to tell the story.
  - It is often good that the editor not be the director. A fresh perspective usually improves a program.
  - Editors usually have more experience in story construction and pacing, because it is their primary task. Directors generally are more occupied with acting, set design, camera movement, and interesting framing, as well as the pacing of the shoot.
- Editing is a complex process, and to be really good requires doing it every day and learning the thousands of adjustable features of digital editing software.
- Editors must learn the syntax and grammar of video editing including techniques like **slow motion**, transitions, color, composites, **parallel action**, flashbacks, etc. to tell the story in a clear, concise, compelling way.

Sony Vegas Pro Video Editing Software Interface

Default layout for Sony Vegas Pro video editing software displaying media library (top left) viewing screens, track controllers(bottom left), time line tracks (bottom right), audio meters (top right).

- Most video editing applications have very similar structural elements, but may use different terms, icons, menu choices, and menu structures to access each. If you learn one well, learning basics of the others is generally easy.
  - o Popular professional software is Final Cut Pro, Sony Vegas Pro, Adobe Premier Pro, Grass Valley Edius, Avid Media Composer, Harris Broadcast Velocity, and Corel Video Studio.
  - o There are many free or cheapo amateur video programs (under $100) that lack most professional level tools. Avoid them.
- **Sony Vegas Pro** is the best because of its affordability, advanced, full features, good-cheap tech support, ease, and speed of use, intuitive time-saving tools, and reliability. It is favored by many independent filmmakers.
  - o Many larger production organizations (TV stations, institutions) use Final Cut Pro, Avid, or Adobe Premier because they made large software and hardware

investments, many years ago, and claim it is too difficult and expensive to change platforms.

- To make yourself marketable as an editor in a large production company, learn Avid or Adobe Premier.
- The more editing programs you know, the better.

o Windows in the interface
- The interface is divided into several windows, mainly: media library, project view window, and timeline.
- Other occasionally used windows are accessible through tabs or menus.
- They include media generator, transition library, audio meters, time clock display, etc.

o Timeline

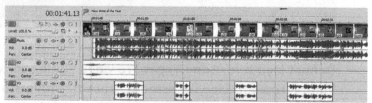

The timeline is the heart of all digital media editors. A cursor travels along the time scale from left to right, playing back the audio and video. The moving video is seen in the project view window.

- The timeline illustrates the order of shots.
- Identifies the image of a clip on a track with text or thumbnail
- Shows type and placement of shot transitions
- Allows working with multiple audio and video tracks.

o Project view window

- A window with a screen where individual frames and sequences of frames are viewed

- **Media library window** displays thumbnail images of all the media in your library.
  - ○ **Post-Edit Ripple Tool**
    - Inserting an event into one or more tracks in a timeline pushes all other selected tracks down the line in sync- on command
    - Best practice is to edit in insert mode, but use post-edit ripple command on all tracks which re-positions all other events down the timeline in sync with the new material.
    - This is a huge time saving tool that should be learned early in the editing process.
  - ○ General interface rules
    - Only the highlighted section is active
    - **Ctrl+Z** undos your last cut
    - Space bar controls play and pause.
    - Interface has a customizable layout.
    - Interfaces can be stretched across two screens, allowing longer view of the program structure with faster access to various tools and features.

Components of Edited Programs

- **Master** and **Close-up** shots

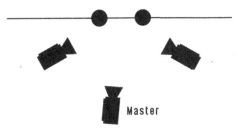

The master shot is a wide shot that covers all the action from one angle. B-Roll, cutaways, or reaction shots are taken from the left and right camera positions.

- Master or establishing shot (A-Roll)
  - ○ The primary content

- o In a documentary, it is interviewee or wide shot of main event being covered
- o In a drama, it is a wide shot that covers all the action
- **B-Roll**
  - o B-roll can be shots that are not related to a master shot, but are called for in script, or discovered by a director or videographer that could assist the editor in creating smooth sequences.
    - Cutaways are Shots related to a master shot, but focused on a particular detail-- object. These are used to enrich the story, objects, people, and places; also to cover cuts.
    - Reaction shots are cutaway shots of people reacting to each other or an event.
  - o Specific types of image content used by editors
    - Original video
    - Videos specially shot for a program
    - **Archival video**
    - Purchased or acquired footage from footage libraries or vendors
    - **Table-top**/insert video- (product close-ups, etc.)
      - Products
      - Props
    - Still photos- possibly with moves **"Ken Burns Effect"**
      - Can be archival
      - Can be obtained from original video frame
    - **Graphics**
      - Graphics general means art work, not live recorded motion video
      - Charts
      - Illustrations/Drawings
      - Animated objects or characters- cartoons
      - Animated backgrounds- usually from a library like Digital Juice

- Text (titles)

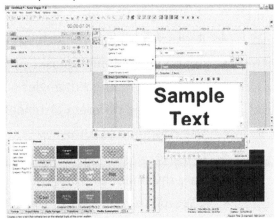

Screen shot of Sony Vegas Pro's Titling window

Editing Work Flow

- o Import video files
  - Importing original captured video from memory cards
  - Still images, other video (from archives, YouTube, etc.)
  - Music or other audio
  - Create specific media folders on drive before importing
  - Important to follow proper media management procedure so shots do not get lost in system
- o Assemble timeline of media events/shots according to script
- o Audio and video are handled independently
- o Separate tracks can be created for similar media, depending on complexity of program: Master, B-roll, graphics, titles, narrator, music, etc.
- o **String out**- assembly of all shots in timeline with more head and tail than needed, in program order
  - Technically unacceptable material is eliminated
  - Generally laid out in story order
- o **Rough cut** – initial edit where shots have been cut down and program shot order and pacing have been established (frequently without transitions)

How to Avoid Jump Cuts When Editing

- Respect **continuity** (match screen content between shots)
- Cut on movement; it masks cut and continuity errors
- Cut between different angles
- Cut between different distances
- Use close-ups as cutaways
- Dissolve, do not cut between zooms
- Vary rhythm of cuts and transitions
- 1 sec. dissolve is a good beginning length
- Cut on still frame at end/beginning of camera move or zoom.

- **Fine cut**- trimming any excess footage; sharpening timing and pacing; inserting transitions; generally the term for a 90% finished project, lacking only titles and music and other audio post.
  - Refine/finalize transitions
    - Transitions connect shots
    - A straight cut is the simplest transition
    - Complex transitions include effect transitions suc dissolves, wipes, page turns, fly-ins and outs, mattes
    - Good, creative transitions take a lot of time
    - Once many transitions are made, it can be difficult to re-edit; finalize them at the end of the edit.

- o **Make visual effects**
    - Compositing (including multiple images on one screen or building sequences from chroma-key shots)

A composite shot includes several images electronically assembled in one frame.

  - **Animation**- image moves around the frame
  - **Crop**- sections at the edges of image are cut to create a cleaner, smaller, or more balanced shot
  - **Zoom** in and out – image changed in size by digitally zooming in or out
  - **Re-position**- digitally moving image within the frame to create a cleaner or more balanced shot.
  - **Fonts-** Create fancy designer type faces
  - Make visual effects after the program's structure has been locked because they can consume a lot of expensive time.
- o **Color-correcting video**
  - **Color correction** means enhancing the color or correcting white balance or exposure errors.
  - Should only be done after picture is locked, so all scenes match; and time not wasted correcting scenes early that don't appear in the program.
- o **"Sweetening"** audio
  - o Reducing or eliminating audio problems
  - o Making volume levels appropriate and consistent throughout tracks
  - o Mixing all tracks into correct stereo or surround sound image

- ○ Making equalization consistent
- ○ Inserting ambient sound or audio efx
- ○ Making audio transitions smooth and accurate

Saving and Rendering Video

- ○ Video projects must be rendered to an audio/video file format viewable outside the editing application, on a media player (DVD, Windows Media Player, Real Player, QuickTime, etc.) Various levels of video quality available
  - Broadcast quality- HD
  - Internet delivery- Highly compressed small files requiring less band width
  - DVD quality- HD
  - **RAM** delivery (digital files on *Random Access Memory* chips for cell phone, tablet). Highly compressed, small files for wireless small screens.
- ○ Most common program file types
  - **.avi** – uncompressed Windows video file, usually for editing only because files are so large
  - **.mov**- apple QuickTime format can be zero compression or highly compressed
  - **.wmv**- for Internet, windows media player playback
  - **.mpeg2**- slight compression for DVD authoring
  - **.mpeg4**- high compression, but good quality
  - **.mts**- AVCHD highly compressed for SDHC flash memory chips
  - Rendering is digital compression that reduces the file size to make it playable on portable devices
  - Rendering makes a copy of the original media files according to the EDL, with all processing complete.
  - Creating the rendered a/v file is a time-consuming process which can take 8-10 times the length of a program.
  - So a one minute program might take eight minutes
    - A ten minute program might take 80 minutes

- Tricked out and tuned computers can render an average in about 2x the run time
- The more complex the timeline, the longer the render time which is determined by
  - Number of video tracks
  - Complexity of transitions
  - Number of composite shots
    - Supers (composite shots)
    - Split-screens
  - Animations
    - Moves, crops, zooms, pans
  - Color corrections and other visual efx
  - Amount of differing detail in the shot (a field of colored flowers

Time code

Time code is created by a time code generator. It displays when each frame was recorded. It does not reflect the time of day, but to a point that refers to the beginning of a particular recording.

- Time code labels each frame with a number. There are 30 frames in a second, then 60 seconds in a minute and 60 minutes in an hour. It looks like this... 10:23:55:27
- Time code only extends to 23 hrs. 59 mins. 59 seconds and 29 frames, then resets to zero. Time code syncs sound and picture from multiple sources.

Multi-camera editing within software

- Useful in sports or live event coverage
- Less expensive and forgiving than live multi-camera shooting and switching
- Some higher end camcorders able to "**jam-sync** together"

Sony Vegas has multi-camera real-time editing capability

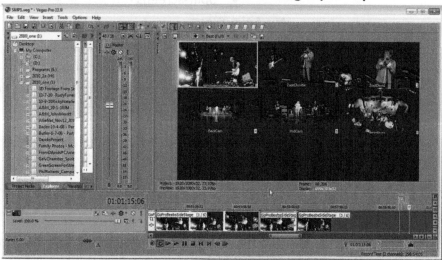

Vegas interface for multi-camera editing. Any of the six tracks seen in the preview window can be selected as they play on the timeline, creating an instantly edited program. Changes are easily made by re-winding and starting again. This is not possible in a program recorded live with a single feed from a switcher.

Miscellaneous Editing Advice

- **Save and Backup**—video tends to crash a lot because it's so demanding on computers. **Save each time you make a change in the project.**
- Match media type with project settings to have the smoothest, clearest playback.
- Keep a notebook at the editing desk to record your favorite project settings, shortcuts, reminders, mathematical calculations, rough drawings
- Use "L" or **lap cuts** (overlap) where sound leads picture or vice-versa, even by just a few frames. It creates momentum. In many cases, it can build very dramatic scenes.
- Keep similar materials on same track; text on one track, all subtitles on one track, graphics on one track, music on one track, each person's dialogue on one track, etc.
- Dissolves cover messy cuts and continuity errors
- Too many dissolves slow the pace; cuts quicken pace
- Too few dissolves make a cold presentation
- The editor's friend is the "**flash frame**," an inserted white frame which covers static jump cuts, especially in interviews; it mimics a camera flash, signaling that there has been a time jump
- When you need to stretch or settle a shaky shot, **slow motion** can be a cure
- Don't overuse music video clichés like black & white scenes, skip frame, scratched film, super-fast cuts, out of focus shots.
- Cutting to Music
    - Cut on the beat
        - Vary cutting on the beat, not always dead on the beat, not always on every beat.
    - Best editors have a good sense of rhythm, like a good musician
        - Editors should understand music theory and mathematical foundation of rhythm
        - 4/4 time ¾ time, etc., rests (beats), counterpoint,

Section 5   Basic Audio for Video

The Importance of Audio
o   You can follow story if picture goes out, but not if sound goes out.
o   Sound must be clear, without distortion, and sufficiently loud.
o   Audio includes speech, sound efx, and music; recorded at different times and require mixing together as separate elements to create a unique "soundtrack."

Microphones

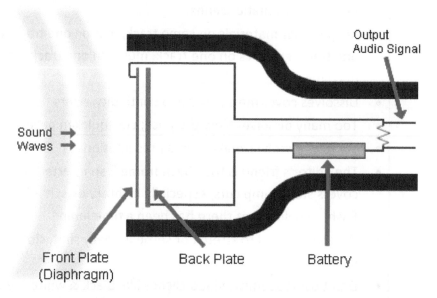

Illustration of a basic microphone design with diaphragm up front. (condenser-see battery).

o   Mics have a diaphragm, like an eardrum, that vibrates in sync with sound waves picked up through the air; a magnet attached to the diaphragm generates tiny electrical pulses. The electrical pulses are transmitted by a cable to a recorder.
o   Primary types of mics
 o   Dynamic
  ▪   Sturdy
  ▪   Do not require electric power
  ▪   Can handle highest sound pressure levels
  ▪   Color the sound because of their mas

- o Condenser
    - Use small amount of electric power that makes them more sensitive (phantom power -48v) from battery pack or preamp.
    - More delicate
- o Microphone care
    - Avoid high temperature
    - Avoid dust/dirt
    - Avoid water/rain/high humidity
    - Avoid shocks
- o Pick-up patterns
    - Omni-directional – all directions
    - Cardioid – heart-shaped (reject off-axis sound, so better recording quality)
    - Supercardioid- elongated heart shape for superior rejection of unwanted sound
- o Mic styles
    - Handheld

This handheld microphone is made by Shure for on-location news assignments, where reliability in difficult circumstances is primary.

- Internally shielded from noise (handling and wind)
- Sturdy
- Not affected by high humidity
- No battery or delicate electronics
- Almost always dynamic mics
- Omnidirectional pick-up pattern, so least critical aiming.
- Cost averages between $80-$150

- Stand mic

- The stand mic is the most common mic used in PA systems and live music. It is sensitive and directional- generally cardioid pattern to reject ambient reverberating sound and speaker feedback.
- Not shielded from handling noise—requires external shock mounts
- Has built in windscreen
- Almost always dynamic mics
- Cost between $80-$200

  o Studio mic

This Avantone mic is a multi-directional studio mic with an external power supply and pre-amp that includes a vacuum tube. Costs about $600.

- Studio mics are generally larger, heavier mics with electronics in the mic body and sometimes, external power supplies and controllers.

- Studio mics are very fragile and sensitive to moisture, shocks, dust, and handling noise, and are rarely used for live performance or field video production.
- Good studio mics prices begin around $350 and can go to $20,000.

o Lavalier

This lavalier mic is mounted in a clip that attaches to a shirt or jacket. It has an XLR connector at the other end.

- Small, attached on clothing
- Condenser mic so needs phantom power, and usually has an integrated battery pack
- Frequently put on musical instruments
- Subject to clothing noise and muffled sound when hidden under clothes

o Shotgun

Audio-Technica Shotgun mic including mounts and custom-fit windscreen. The slits on the side allow sound from behind the mic to be phase reversed and therefore reduced in volume. "Shotgun" relates to shape, not pick-up pattern.

- Shotgun mics are used in noisy locations because they reject ambient sound.
- Sensitive condenser mic
- Can pick up well several feet away from subject.
  o Wireless mics – use high quality, small transmitters and receivers instead of cables.

Wireless mic kit including: transmitter for hand-held mic(l), wearable transmitter with lavalier mic(m), receiver(r).

- Convenient
- Transmitter be bulky under wardrobe
- Usually lavalier style but also hand-held models
- Receiver can add bulk to camera
- Require many batteries
- Fragile, easily lost
- Can be subject to electrical/radio wave interference
- Have limited range
- Proper mic positioning
  - 6 inches from mouth is best, but up to 36 inches works depending on mic pick-up pattern, ambient noise, volume of the source.

Proper mic position: mic aimed directly at mouth, distance 6"

- On boom – when needs to be hidden
    - Overhead or underneath, depending on shot composition
    - Easy to control to follow movement
- On stand – floor or desk stand
    - Usually only if visible as part of setting, or voice over recordings
- Microphone Accessories
    - Cables
        - Professional mics use XLR connectors
        - ¼" phone connectors
        - Mini phone connectors
    - Windscreens

Windscreens slow down or stop ambient air bursts from entering the mic and making a distorted rumbling sound. They have different shapes and styles, and designed to stop wind noise without interfering with the sound.

- Foam (see above)- Most mics have custom-fit foam windscreens included in their package.

- o Windsock

    - made of fluffy material that fits over the foam screen to make a greater barrier to stronger wind gusts.
- o Spit/Pop screen

    - used only in studios to limit plosive consonant sounds (b,p) by vocalists; also filters spit/saliva projected by many lively singers. Pop screen material can be washed or cheaply replaced when it gets too gross.
- Shock mounts/Handling noise

Mic mounted in a shock mount.
- o Suspended- with elastic shock absorbing bands
- o Built-into hand-held mics, so handling noise is greatly reduced

- Carrying cases
  - Protection from elements (heat, moisture, dirt)
- Boom poles

Boom or Fish poles are poles with a mic mounted on one end; they allow a boom operator to get close to the actors without interfering with action or camera.

- Fish poles – are handheld and meant for light weight mics with 3-9 ft. max reach
- Are used in-studio or on location

Other audio equipment

Field mic mixers

This small, rugged and reliable location sound mixer for video costs more than $3,000. Mixers of lower quality cost only a few hundred dollars; they can get the job done, but are fragile.

- Battery operated
- Connected to camera by cable or wireless
- Sometimes connected to outboard recorder
- 2-5 input channels x 2 outputs
- Few signal processing capabilities besides volume, or fixed filters
- Have only 1 or 2 output channel choices

Audio monitors

- Headphones
  - On-camera speakers- very poor quality; use headphones for playback
  - Over-the-ear headphones block ambient sound.

- Loudspeakers- come in all sizes from 1/8" (cellphone) to 15"(stadium PA or electric bass)

Audio level meters

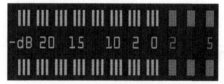

  - Meters are dynamic scales that show minimum and maximum levels of audio, measured in decibels (db)
  - Peak reading meters-LED - Show only peak volume
  - Often have 3 colors: green (safe level), yellow (safe, but do not exceed), red (bad, sound will probably be distorted
  - In camcorders may only be white dots with a mark where distortion may occur.

Main audio connector types

  - XLR- balanced, professional grade used for mic input

XLR Male Connector has 3 pins and a latch to lock it securely to the socket.

- TRS- balanced or unbalanced single shaft with multiple pick-up areas on the shaft.

TRS Male Connector has one pin with several sections and a spring latch system

- Mini-phone connectors pro-sumer, consumer grade, unbalanced, more susceptible to electronic noise; most commonly used in camcorders for headphones out only.
- They function like TRS connector, but are much smaller and used in phones, personal portable music players, and other consumer-oriented devices
- **See *Common Connector Illustrated Sheet* at end of book for more connectors.**

Solving common recording problems

- Hard, reflective conditions
    - Create multiple echoes that muddy sound- "reverberations"
    - Require treatments like
        - Foam panels
        - Sound blankets to deaden sound

Sound blankets are "moving blankets." They are cheap, durable solutions to high reverb locations. The can be put on floors or hung from light stands.

- o Avoid "live" empty rooms to reduce reverb
  - ▪ furnishings like carpet, drapes, padded furniture, acoustical tile ceiling help
  - ▪ close mic placement helps
- ▪ Noisy conditions
  - o Consistent non-interruptible- Factories, heavy traffic, windy, moving water, large crowds, music
  - o Consistent interruptible- mainly refrigerator, HVAC
  - o Airplane passing overhead, loud truck passing, lawn mower workers, thunder/rain
- • Need to choose site carefully
- • Use close mic placement
- • Work between unavoidable location sounds (airplanes, emergency vehicle sirens)
  - o Ask sound source to be quiet for a short time
- • Mics on overhead booms can cast a distracting shadow on the back wall of a set.

Mic and boom shadows on background walls are an annoyance.
- o To lessen the problem, choose from under or above mic placement; under usually works best.
- o Work with lights to flag lights, add shadow eleminating lights, or soften light.
- o Use hidden or body mic

Anticipating editorial needs for sound
- • Keep volume levels consistent
- • Keep mic position consistent to preserve tonal quality
- • Keep mic model consistent
- • Avoid mic handling noise

- Stop unnecessary ambient sound (lawn mowers, refrigerators, car motors)
- Record separate ambient sound or "room tone"
- Record 2 person interviews with 2 mics routed to separate channels

Audio in the TV Studio

The audio control room in a TV studio is separate from the video control room so audio doesn't interfere with the director. In small installations without a separate audio control room, audio engineer must use headphones.

- TV studio mics are connected to a patch panel in the studio, then routed to console in the TV audio control room.
- Lavalier mics are the primary studio mic, but some talk shows may use desk stands.
- Live musicians use floor mic stands or mics on booms.
- The TV studio audio engineer sets uptudio mics, and runs cbles to the proper patch panels.
    - Wireless mics and intercoms are the responsibility of the audio engineer.
    - Assistant audio engineers may be situated in the studio to adjust mics and troubleshoot while the engineer stays in the control room.

- Live TV audio is an advanced technical job that requires managing multiple live studio mics, audio from outside program feeds (satellite), and playback from recordings.
- The TV studio audio engineer is in intercom contact with the director who feeds upcoming audio changes.
- The studio audio engineer is responsible for clear, consistent volume levels fed to the recorder. Studio audio should not be cluttered with studio background noise, electronic noise, echo, or feedback.

Section 6 Directing Tips

Shooting Process

Storyboards

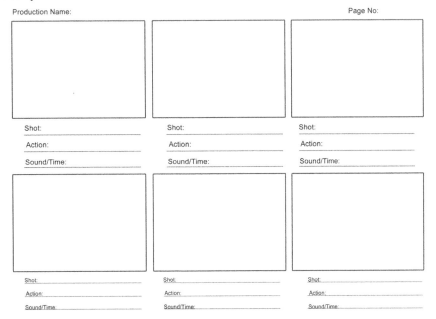

Storyboard blank page ready to be filled in with illustrations.

o   Storyboards are hand or computer drawn illustrations used in planning shooting sequences; they show how each scene should be composed, and how it connects with other scenes. They can be rough pencil sketches or precise CGI images.

Shot coverage

o   Interviews
  - Beginning should be 2-shot
  - Close up of interviewee answering all questions
  - Close up of interviewer asking all questions
  - Shoot reaction shots of both: nodding head slightly, looking ahead
  - Shoot cutaway close-ups of interviewer taking notes
  - Shoot cutaway close-ups of both sets of hands

- Event coverage
    - Master shots – wide angles of the action
    - Cutaways or "B-roll"
    - Extreme close-ups of detailed actions or objects
    - Close-up and medium shots of individuals

- Dramas
    - Master shot/establishing shot
    - Close-ups of all dialogue
    - Reaction shots of all dialogue
    - Spiced up with
        - Over the shoulder shots
        - Odd angles
        - 2-shots
        - Point-of-view
        - Close-ups and extreme close-ups of details
- Sports
    - Wider is better so extreme and surprise movements can be seen in relation to field or stage position and relationship with other players

Shooting out of sequence

- shooting from one camera set-up all scripted material that requires coverage from that angle or on that set or location
- This material could occur at different times and places in the script
- Shooting out of sequence allows doing one production set-up and all that it entails like set dressing, talent, special equipment, etc.

Screen direction

o   Crossing the line or **180 degree rule**

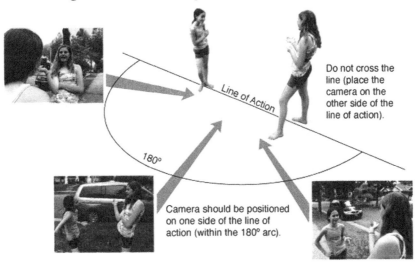

Line of Action

Do not cross the line (place the camera on the other side of the line of action).

180°

Camera should be positioned on one side of the line of action (within the 180° arc).

A good illustration of how to maintain consistent eye lines.

o   Maintaining correct screen direction and eye-line, by positioning camera so that talent always look in the right direction. It can get confusing because screens are 2-dimensional and normal spatial cues can be absent in tight shots coverage.

o   Talent should always be looking at the same side of the frame. When cameras cross the 180 line, they start looking at the opposite side of the camera; it's as if when you're conversing with someone you jump the line, and they have to keep turning their head to follow you.

o   In covering sports, all cameras should be on one side of the field.

Qualities of good shots

o   Proper exposure (brightness/contrast)

o   Correct Color

o   Proper Focus

o   Clear, robust audio

o   Camera Movement

o   Steady camera (except for dramatic effects)

o Generally need 3-5 seconds still head and tail before any movement (pre-roll)

o Always plan where to begin and end move, rehearse, if possible

Backgrounds

o Use neutral backgrounds that do not distract from main subject

o Keep backgrounds in softer focus by using a longer lens and taking advantage of depth of field differences.

- Do not allow strong lines or shapes to intersect or interact with main objects e.g. a flagpole in the background that appears at the top of a person's head could look like it is growing out of the top of the head.

Mottled printed canvas background

- Wrinkled vari-tonal canvas sheets are common backgrounds used in studios that are cheap and don't create compositional problems, especially if they are shot slightly out of focus

- When conducting interviews, consider the background; choose a neutral or meaningful, like bookshelves; manipulate background or other objects in set to make a good background, but return them to original after finished.

Basic shooting tips

> ### Basic Shooting Tips for the Videographer/Director
>
> 1. Provide sufficient lead room.
> 2. Provide sufficient head room.
> 3. Place eyes or principal subject/object at a third generally.
> 4. All camera moves and zooms should be smooth.
> 6. Plan shot before shooting.
> 7. Shot should have a beginning, middle, and end.
> 8. Rehearse shots whenever you can.
> 9. Moving shots should have a 2 second still beginning, run at least 5 seconds, and have a 2 second hold at the end.
> 10. Set exposure and white balance with every camera setup.
> 11. Set initial focus by zooming in fully and racking focus in and out until sharpest image is achieved.
> 12. Check that zebra is set at 95%
> 13. Subjects/objects should be facing the sun.
> 14. Backgrounds should not be brighter than the subject.
> 15. Backgrounds should be softer focus than central object.

Running the Shoot

Director commands

- Everybody ready? (about to shoot- speak up if problem)
- Standby (to record)
- Roll (record now)
- Action (begin performance)
- Cut (stop performance, stop camera)
- Re-set (prepare to do another take immediately)
- Take 5 (Take a short break) OK to leave position for 3-4 minutes—restroom break, drink, phone call
- Wrap (break down equipment for end of day or move set-up if "wrap location")

Working with talent

- Talent should walk in and walk out of moving shots
- Give specific directions when suggesting changes, give reasons why performance was not good; not "try it again a different way" instead say "do it a little faster, and look at the glass when you say the wine is good"
- Hire the talented people; they make you look good.
- Let talent do their job. Most bad acting is due to bad casting.

Camera set-up

- A new camera set-up is a new camera position
- Can be to get another take of the same scene, or move to a different scene
- Usually requires changing lights, sound position, and props to accommodate camera movement
- Sometimes talent is added or changed.

Camera takes

- recording from the same position (setup) the same piece from the script
- no major changes
- takes will be repeated until a good one has been achieved and then director calls to move to the next **set-up**
- a good director knows when he/she has obtained the best effort of everyone involved, and not wasted time with extra unneeded takes
- sometimes a "protection shot" is done in case there's a technical glitch—like an accidental erasure, or there's a problem that was noticed on set.
- Do not keep shooting takes, looking for impossible perfection; it exhausts everyone's patience and breaks the budget.

Studio Multi-camera Shooting

Multi-camera production deserves a book of its own, but a quick overview of its components follows:

- o Multiple cameras can be used to cover events like sports, parades, conventions, performances, newscasts and talk shows.
- o Cameras are live-switched through a **video switcher**
- o Additional non-camera sources can run through switcher including multiple: graphics, video playback, satellite, Internet material, and remote broadcast feeds.
- o All live cameras and sources must be synced to same master clock.
- o Audio is controlled and switched via a separate mixer.
- o Single audio-video program stream is output through the switcher to broadcast and/or recorder
- o Some cameras may be recorded individually for later editing
- o Most live programs also have a live program feed
- o Large sporting events can use up to 30 cameras simultaneously
- o Classic studio set-up is three cameras, which can cover the minimal number of angles for a smoothly cutting program.

Directing live multi-camera television is a difficult, unique skill requiring sharp mental focus quick-thinking, good memory, good sense of visual rhythm, good organizational skills, and a cool head (check out **video director samples on YouTube**)

A large television network control room with dozens of incoming video sources.

Section 7   Producing

Proposals, Treatments, Scripts

Proposals

o   Proposal sells the concept
- Short description of the project to generate initial interest
- Answers Who, what, when, where, why
- Defines audience
- Target cost/budget for major categories
- Production team names
- Proposals are not paid work

o   Treatments
- o Treatment is first production step
- o Treatments are paid work
- o Describe the structure and content in a narrative/essay form
  - Story
  - Locations
  - Interviewees/Talent

- Events covered
- Illustrative material
- Archival material

Script breakdown (*see "Lists and Forms" section for sample*)

o Script breakdowns are generally used on dramatic productions, but can be helpful in non-fiction films that use numerous props, locations, vehicles, objects, talent.

o The script breakdown is a list of all the products, services and personnel required in the script, so a budget can be created; these are compiled scene by scene from the script and include

  o Studio rental
  o Location rental
  o Art Dept purchases and rentals of
    - Props
    - Sets
    - Expendable supplies
      - Lumber
      - Paint
      - Adhesives
      - Cleaning
      - Wallpaper
      - Prop food
  o Hair & Makeup including purchases and rentals of
    - Expendable supplies
      - Makeup
      - Cleaning supplies
      - Hairspray
      - Paper towels
    - Special Equipment
  o Wardrobe including purchases and rentals of
    - Costumes
    - Special services like laundry and repair
    - Equipment like storage racks, sewing machines

- o Crew personnel
  - All working persons on the set or contributing items to the set
- o Administrative personnel
- o People working in the office providing administrative support.

Schedule estimate

- A schedule is created after the script is final to determine the most efficient order of shooting scenes to minimize the amount of time and travel required of the products and personnel used in the production.
- Scheduling follows the practice of shooting out of story sequence, but in location/set sequence to minimize the number of times a set, prop, actor, etc. needs to be re-used.
- The fewer days an item is used, the lower its cost, and so the budget can be lower. Most items are charged for on a time used basis; e.g. how many days a camera is needed, how many days an actor is required on set.

Money management & budgeting

Overview of budgeting

- o A Sample Budget is in the *Lists & Forms Section*
- o A budget is a comprehensive list of all the costs of making a production from concept through final delivery
- o The list is categorized by company departments; e.g. cast, camera, catering, etc.
- o Current item costs are found through research, and are frequently negotiable.
- o Many budget forms exist, some in computer applications that include long pre-set lists of products and services
- o Several budget programs automate the process
- o Global changes in the budget can be made simply by changing these key amounts enabling quick multiple budget versions

using "what if?" scenarios such is "What if we shoot non-union?" What if we only shoot "30 days instead of 35?"

- o Fundraising
  - Requires a proposal package
    - o Most productions use the treatment, script and budget as primary documents
    - o Many will include biographies of key personnel
- o Legal and insurance
  - Legal contracts are required to be sure all permissions have been obtained, and all personnel are bound to the production
  - Insurance protects the investment in case natural disasters, error or neglect, or loss or damage to original video requiring a re-shoot. Insurance also protects all equipment or personnel against injury or damage during the production.
- o Production elements and crew Included in budget
  - Production
  - Production management
    - Producer
    - Production Manager/Coordinator
    - Production Assistants
    - Production Auditor
    - Director
    - Assistant Director(s)
  - Technical crew
    - Camera
    - Lighting/grip
    - Sound
  - Art Departments
    - Scenic
    - Make-up & Wardrobe
    - Special EFX
    - Props & Sets
  - Cast/Talent
    - Star flat rates

- Weekly
- Day players
- Extras
- Production equipment rental and purchase
  - Sometimes extensive amounts of equipment is rented for just a day, or many months
  - Sometimes it pays to own your own equipment, depending on the long-term rental cost
  - Production expendable supplies
    - Include gaffers tape, rope, office supplies, bulbs,
- Transportation
  - Sometimes vans and trucks need to be rented to haul large amounts of rented lighting and other equipment
- Locations
  - Require scouting and legal restrictions
  - Rental terms
  - Repairs, relocation expense, loss of income
  - Permits
  - Some sites require government permits and liability if there is damage or injury, the insurance company will pay
- Crafts service and meals- catering and cleaning
- Better to supply food to crew at once in one place rather than have everybody leave set and run into delays.
  - Shooting schedule
    - Based on budgeting schedule
    - Changes daily based on weather problems, technical delays, slow workers
    - Use computer and **strip board**
  - Cost accounting/tracking
    - Actual costs entered into accounting program and compared to budgeted amounts to see if production is on budget

- o All costs need to be documented with receipts, invoices, or contracts
- o Post-production
  - o Video editing
  - o Voice/narrator/actor recording
  - o Graphics production
  - o Audio/Music editing, production
- o Distribution and marketing
  - o Distributors specialize in selling your production to various markets around the world.
  - o Distributors generally charge 80% of gross income for their services.
  - o Marketing, or informing people about your production is critical to its success, and should be considered before deciding a project is worth producing.

Top 20 Producer's Organizational Skills

1. Carry writing instrument and pad or computer for notes.
2. Write everything down; if you use sticky notes, quickly transfer them to your to-do list.
3. Make business cards and carry them always.
4. Always carry your cell phone.
5. Get a hands-free bag to carry books, tapes, notes, camera, flash or hard drives, other office supplies.
6. Be expert in MS Word, Excel and Outlook.
7. Keep contacts and calendar information up to date with Outlook or Google or similar.
8. Have reliable car with plenty of gas.
9. Make a good impression-look like the people you're working with (or who you want to work with).
10. Be 8 minutes early to all appointments (sooner makes you look pushy, later makes you look disorganized).
11. Be positive- never say no, never give excuses (but promise you'll never make the same mistake again).
12. Acknowledge/return all phone calls and other messages within 30 minutes.
13. Put personal ID tags on all of your items (phone, hard drive, carry case, computer) in case they're left somewhere.
14. Have a credit card for ID and emergency purchases.
15. Know cost-tracking software like Quicken or QuickBooks.
16. Have a business bank account.
17. Build a network of people in the business to expand resources and opportunities—it's a heavily freelance business.
18. Promote/brand yourself with social media and website.

Tips for money management

o Create a budget—learn to use MS Excel

o Keep receipts for everything

o Pay your income taxes

o Cost tracking – Is the accounting process that shows how much the production has cost to date, and how much it will cost based on actual completed purchases and signed contracts and budget estimates, which can vary due to fluctuating prices or production problems.

o Cost tracking helps make informed adjustments that will enable completion of production on budget

o Most financers of large productions want to see regular cost-tracking reports to be sure film can be completed on budget.

o Use Quicken or commercial accounting software

o Independent contractors in the production world may deduct many career-related things like cell phone, Internet, car mileage, meals, video rental, pay TV, movie tickets, certain clothing, travel, certain amount of rent of mortgage, office supplies, video and audio equipment.

o Independent contractors bill for their work; they are not on payroll with tax deductions.

o Having a corporation generally puts you in a better tax situation and can save thousands of tax dollars a year.

o Have a professional tax preparer experienced with independent contractors working in the arts do your taxes.

Essential Video Terms

Camera/Shooting

1. Zoom (action, lens) – magnification of image by adjusting lens elements to vary focal length and give the impression of camera movement closer or further from the object being shot
2. White balance- adjusting video electronics to set a baseline for "pure white" to match the ambient light's color temperature
3. Focus- sharpness of an image
4. Rack focus- changing focus from one focal plane to another
5. Depth of field- the depth of area that is in apparent focus
6. Focal length- the size of a lens; it determines the amount of magnification; the larger the focal length, the more the magnification, and the longer the lens is
7. Iris- controls the amount of light allowed to register on the image processor; it controls the exposure level from brightest to black
8. Aperture- same as iris
9. Shutter speed- the amount of time the pick-up chip is activated to record one image frame
10. Automatic gain control- automatic adjustment of iris and shutter to provide a consistent exposure level
11. Auto iris- same as automatic gain control; except controls iris only, not shutter
12. Gain- an electronic circuit that boosts the light level from the camera's image processor; used in dark situations; usually results in degradation of the image that cannot be changed; in critical low-light situations it's use is acceptable.
13. Blocking- planning the placement of objects and/or people in your shot, before recording
14. Pan- moving the camera side to side (horizontally)
15. Tilt- moving the camera up and down (vertically)
16. Tripod- supports the camera and pan head
17. Base plate- connects the camera to the pan head
18. Pan head- supports camera and allows smooth tilting and zooming when moved with a handle

19. CCD-charge-coupled device; the light-sensitive pick-up chip in a video camera
20. Color bars- graphic still with several basic colors used to adjust the camera to a standard color reference
21. Color temperature- the particular color of a light source; all sources have different color temperatures, and emit different colors—sunlight, tungsten lights, fluorescent, LED, etc.
22. Drop frame/non-drop frame- A type of counting of frames when recording video
23. Time code- a specific address of a frame of video using hours, minutes, seconds, and frames that is embedded in the video signal; a necessity for editing video
24. Close-up- highly magnified image of a person or object
25. Medium shot- less magnified image of a person or object
26. Wide shot- much less magnified image of a person or object
27. Two-shot- two persons included in a shot, as in shooting a 2-person interview
28. Master shot- wide shot that includes all the action of a specific shot
29. Frames per second- the rate at which video frames are recorded usually 24, 25, or 29.9 (30) that results in the illusion of motion due to persistence of vision; the more frames per second, the sharper the image. Some cameras experiment with 60+ fps
30. Head room- leaving space at the top of a frame of an image
31. Lead room- leaving space at the left or right of an image, especially when the object/person is moving, or in the case of a close-up of a person, in the direction the person is looking
32. Image stabilization- Electronic or optical-mechanical process to reduce shaky camera images; it can also be done in some editing software
33. Menu- list of digital camera adjustments that can be made using software within the camera
34. Mic connector- receptacle on the camera to plug in a mic or mic cable
35. Pan handle- Handle on the tripod/pan head used to control pan and tilt movements of the camera
36. Over/under exposure- Excessively bright image that exceeds the technical limits of the camera's pick-up chips resulting in washed-out de-saturated colors; insufficient light to see details, proper colors or contrast.

37. White card- a pure white card used as the subject when adjusting the white balance of the camera
38. Rule of thirds- to create the most pleasing standard composition, the eyes should align with the top-third horizontal line of the frame.
39. Screen direction- the direction a subject is looking or moving
40. Shot- a single event recorded on camera where the camera begins recording and then stops.
41. Set-up- a single spot from which several shots may be taken, but the camera is not moved between takes
42. Polarizer- a filter that cuts most glare from a shot making it clearer and crisper; it also reduces brightness and works best in bright sunlight
43. ND filter- "neutral density" filter-a filter that reduces light entering the lens by using a glass filter that is tinted a color-neutral gray filter.

Editing

1. Crossing the line- shooting a subject from two angles so that when edited together, they appear to be mirror images of each other
2. Fade- slowly reducing image brightness from normal to black as a digital effect
3. Dissolve- fading in an image over another that is fading out so that the new image replaces the old
4. Cut- Changing from one shot to another on an exact frame line, so the change appears instant and uninterrupted.
5. Transition- Changing from one shot to another by overlapping the end/beginning of the shot creating a superimposition; hundreds of variable transitions are available in editing software; dissolve is the most basic transition
6. Render- Processing edited shots into a final program consisting of a single file playable on a playback device that includes all the images, graphics, and audio of the program built in the timeline.
7. B-roll- Shots taken for a program that support the primary shots, by allowing cutting away from the primary shots eliminate jump cuts
8. Media folder- place on the hard drive where video shots are stored; no editing information is stored in a media folder
9. .avi- Windows audio/video file type; this is the uncompressed, highest quality video file.

10. .wmv- Compressed Windows audio/video file type playable primarily on Windows Media Player, suitable for playing on a computer or transmission over the Internet or ethernet

11. .mov- Compressed Apple QuickTime audio/video file playable primarily on QuickTime Players; for playing on a computer or over the Internet; .mov has various levels of compression, including uncompressed.

12. .fla or .flv- Compressed Adobe Flash audio/video file type; playable only on Flash Players; suitable for playing on a computer or transmission over the Internet or ethernet

13. .mpg(1) (2) (4) Compressed audio/video file types that are playable on many different media players, at various quality levels, from very high to very low.

14. Dub- a complete copy of a video program; on DVD or Hard drive

15. Jump cut- a cut between shots that leaves out part of the recorded sequence; it creates a jarring sensation that can distract or enhance the program flow, depending on how it is used, or misused.

16. Sweetening- adjusting the audio in a video program with EQ, volume, compression and special effects to change its original qualities.

Studio Production

1. Character generator- software that creates on-screen text in a video editing or switching system

2. Pedestal- Equipment that holds studio cameras; like a tripod in the field, but allows smooth up and down movement of the camera, and wheels to roll smoothly across the floor.

3. Chroma key- Electronically eliminating a specific color in an image and replacing it with a different image

4. Control room- The room near the studio where all the cameras and audio are controlled and mixed with other sources to produce and record a specific program.

5. Teleprompter- Apparatus in front of a camera lens that projects text on a slightly mirrored glass that can be viewed by read by talent looking directly into the camera lens, so the reading looks natural and not scripted.

6. Intercom- Studio communications system connecting audio, cameras, teleprompter etc. to director

7. Switcher- console that selects specific video feeds to be routed to transmitter or recorder; can be from cameras, computer graphic stations, video network, satellite, Internet, or video playback; some switchers can be digital computer applications controlled with a mouse and keyboard
8. Audio snake- collection of audio cables coming from a central patch panel and leading to audio input console
9. Lighting grid- poles mounted from the ceiling of a studio where lighting instruments are attached; usually has multiple electrical outlets leading to dimmer/control system
10. Grip equipment- stands and mounts specifically designed to support and control lighting equipment and accessories.

Lighting

1. Backlight- defines subject from background by creating highlights on shoulders
2. Key light- defines principal direction from which lighting is coming; provides interest to shot
3. Fill light- all other light hitting subject besides the key light; usually slightly less bright and smooth
4. Contrast ratio- the difference between the darkest and brightest portions of an image
5. Cucalorus (cookie) – large panel with random shapes cut out and placed in front of a light that projects abstract shapes if light on a background (looks like sunlight filtering through leaves on a tree) to give texture and dimension to the background, thus adding interest.
6. Cutter- a thin, sharp edged object placed in front of a light that blocks a portion of the light, keeping it off un-wanted portions of a scene.
7. Flag- similar to a cutter, but often used to shade the camera lens from unwanted excess light to avoid lens flares
8. Grip stand/"C" stand- miscellaneous stand, usually with three legs used to hold cookies, flags, and cutters.
9. Dimmer- an electronic device that raises or lowers voltage feed to light thereby brightening or dimming the lighting output
10. Flat lighting- lighting that has no shadows
11. High key lighting- lighting that creates hard shadows

12. Barn door- small flat adjustable panels on a lighting unit that block light from hitting a certain area of the scene being shot
13. Scrim- a metal screen inserted in front of a light that reduces amount of light emitted by the unit.
14. Gel holder- on a lighting unit, a frame in that attaches to the front of the instrument and affects the light output, to hold
15. Gel- tinted plastic sheet that changes the color of the light
16. Diffusion material- plastic sheet that is translucent and therefore scatters and softens the light
17. Fresnel Lens- An element of sculpted glass in front of the bulb that evenly concentrates the light into a specific, sharply defined area, magnifying the light output of the instrument.

Essential Audio Terms for Video

1. Microphone- picks up sound and creates an electronic signal
2. Boom- holds a microphone overhead
3. Automatic level control- automatically adjusts volume to pre-determined level to limit distortion
4. Level control- manually adjusts volume or gain
5. Channel selector- allows audio to be routed to unique audio channel
6. Attenuator- lowers volume a specific amount
7. Phantom power- supplies 48 volt power to condenser mics
8. Off mic- low volume, low-quality recording due to performer not being close enough or in front of the microphone
9. Directional mic- cancels unwanted sounds that are off axis to the microphone's main pickup pattern
10. dB- Decibel- unit of measurement of sound volume/level
11. Balanced connections- Balanced reduces electronic noise with a flexible shield around the main conductor wires
12. Distortion- Audio level is too high, reducing clarity and accuracy of recording due to exceeding mic and pre-amplifier capabilities
13. XLR connector- professional connector for balanced applications; they have a positive locking mechanism to hold them in place
14. RCA connector- non-professional, unbalanced connector for line-level applications like pre-amplifiers or speakers

15. Mini-phone connector- space saving 1/8" connector for small audio recorders/players like i-pods or non-professional computer speakers/inputs
16. Audio level meter- gives graphic representation of audio signal volume using LEDs or dynamic needle/pointer and dB scale

Video Production Work Flow

1. Camera
    a. Proper preparation
        i. Battery
            i. Seat battery properly
            ii. Check battery charge level
        ii. Viewfinder diopter set
            i. Adjust diopter focus lever so set for your eye
        iii. SDHC chip properly loaded
            i. Label chip
            ii. Record/safe switch set to record
            iii. Chip inserted into chip slot
            iv. Chip slot door shut firmly
        iv. Tripod set, level and camera attached
            i. Legs extended and firmly locked
            ii. Attach camera using camera base plate
            iii. Level using camera level
            iv. Loosen pan and tilt locks
    b. Camera settings
        i. Set to manual control
            i. Slide switch to "manual"
        ii. Zebra on
            i. Push Zebra button so "Zebra 90 %" appears on lcd screen
        iii. Correct shutter speed
            i. Push iris/shutter dial to shutter setting; dial to 1/60 setting
        iv. Correct iris/gain setting
            i. Push iris/shutter dial to iris setting; turn dial until zebra lines begin to appear on brightest sections of your primary subject (not background)
        v. White balance
            i. Hold a white object in front of your subject

      ii.   Zoom in on the white object until only white appears.

      iii.   Push and hold white balance button approximately 3 seconds, or until white balance icon appears (screen will go black for a second or two)

c. Camera operation

   i. Focus set

      i.   Zoom- in to your subject fully

      ii.   Turn focus ring slowly until subject is sharp focus, and go beyond slightly

      iii.   Reverse focus ring very slowly to bring focus into sharpest image

      iv.   Zoom out and compose subject properly, with best focus assured

   ii. Smooth zoom in/out movement

      i.   Press zoom rocker switch gently for slow zoom; the less pressure used, the slower the zoom

      ii.   Begin and end all moves from a still position

   iii. Smooth pan and tilt movements

      i.   Begin all moves from a still position

      ii.   Turn zoom handle slowly and at as constant speed as possible (this can take a lot of practice)

      iii.   Begin and end from a still position

   iv. Focus and other settings maintained

      i.   Handle camera carefully; do not accidently push or move and dials or switches

   v. Proper balanced composition

      i.   Eyes at a third

      ii.   Appropriate headroom

      iii.   Do not crop important elements of the shot

      iv.   Avoid unnecessary and distracting elements (flag pole stuck in head)

      v.   Appropriate leading in moving and still shots

   vi. Sufficient shot length and variety

      i.   Head and tail – 2 seconds minimum still

      ii.   Duration – 5 seconds minimum is best

         iii.   Vary angles or add slight movements (zoom in/out-pan/tilt)

2. Using Sony Vegas Pro or other digital video editing software
   a. Set up project folder
      i. Create in non-program drive; give clear, detailed name
      ii. Copy files from camera to hard drive
   b. Import video files to project media library
   c. Import audio files to project media library (eg. music, voice-over)
   d. Set up workspace
      i. Generally use default
   e. Add video to timeline
      i. Double-click or drag from library
   f. Make clean cuts
      i. Do not leave unneeded video frames that distract
      ii. Do not cut needed audio frames
   g. Perform basic transitions
      i. Dissolves and wipes
   h. Create graphic/title track
      i. Create graphics and titles
   i. Adjust audio levels and clarity
   j. Adjust video brightness and color
   i. Render program to appropriate playback file type

Section 8   Video Lists and Forms

Lists and forms are important elements in learning and carrying out video production.

They help ensure that you will not forget critical steps.

They are handy reference guides when editing or writing. Treat them as your personal assistant.

Keep them in your notebook, phone, computer, touch pad, and tacked to the bulletin board above your desk or workstation.

Use the following lists and forms to assist in pre-production.

Vegas Cheat Sheet

1 hr. of original HD video is about 16 Gb

Keyboard Shortcuts:

Space Bar: Start/Stop

S: Cut

Ctl+Z: Undo previous action

Ctl+Y: Re-do previous action

G: Group selected tracks

U: Ungroup selected tracks

X: Solo selected tracks

M: Insert marker

J,K,L Transport Control: L=forward 1x, 1.5x, 2x, 4x; K= stop; J=reverse 1x, 1.5x, 2x, 4x

V: View volume envelope

P: View pan envelope

Shft+Ctl+F: Post-edit Ripple on all tracks

F: Post-edit Ripple on selected tracks only

Ctl+F: Post-edit Ripple on all affected tracks

#1 & #3 Move cursor 1 frame back or 1 frame forward; hold to play

#4 & #6 Move cursor 4 frames back or 4 frames forward

#7 Jump to head of next clip

#9 Jump to head then end of next clip

Home: Go to beginning of time line or selection

Ctrl+End: Go to end of time line

Tab: Select Audio or Video or Both in Trimmer

Clip use count: Project media> Detailed view

Field Shoot Checklist

1. Camera Kit
   a. Prep Cases
   b. 1 or 2 charged batteries
   c. Charger and AC cable
   d. SDHC Cards (3 checked)
   e. Windscreens
   f. White card
   g. Camera-tripod base plate
   h. Tripod
   i. Check all menu settings (see list below)
   j. Sharpie
   k. Lens cap
   l. UV filter
   m. Polarizer
   n. Lens cleaning cloth
   o. Lens adapters- Wide& Tele
   p. Final Camera Check (SDHC card loaded, record bars, audio levels, playback)
2. Grip/Light
   a. Extension cords
   b. 3:2 A/C adapter
   c. Gaffer Tape
   d. Tool Kit
   e. A/C Cube tap/power strip
   f. Make-up kit
   g. Reflector
   h. Steadicam
   i. Light Kit
   j. Extra light bulbs
   k. Cart needed?
3. Audio
   a. External mic (condenser or dynamic)
   b. Headphones/earbuds
   c. Mic fish pole
   d. Wireless mics
   e. AA batts for wireless mics
   f. Back-up hand mic
   g. Mic cable
   h. Audio adapter pack for location PA tap
4. Personal
   a. Carry Pack/Backpack
   b. Sunhat/sunscreen/bug spray/first aid
   c. Rain Cover/poncho/jacket
   d. Water/snack
   e. Cell phone charged
   f. Pocket change/cash
   g. Notepad and pen
   h. Contact info/maps
   i. Trash bag
   j. Car keys protected

Camera Menu Settings
   k. Zebra on- 95%
   l. Auto/Manual focus set
   m. Manual mode set
   n. ND filter set
   o. Iris correct
   p. 1/60 shutter speed
   q. 30 fps camera speed
   r. Resolution (720p)
   s. Mic mixer set
      i. ATT off
      ii. Channel selection correct
      iii. Phantom on/off
      iv. Good level set
      v. Second mic level 0db
      vi. Mixer plugged into camera
      vii. Test with headphones

Video Recording Service Request Form

Please complete to the best of your knowledge then submit this form to _____.
We will call back to discuss set up issues.
Contact

Client contact name:
Client Organization:
Phone Number:
Email:

Date of event:

Planned Start and end Time:

Estimated duration of presentation and Q&A:

Address:

What is the space like (classroom, auditorium, about how many seats)?:

Briefly describe the event:

Can we get access to the room 1 hour before presentation begins for set-up?

How many people will speak?

Will a PA system be used?

Will the speaker use a podium or move around?

Will the speaker(s) use a wireless hand mic or wireless lavalier?

Will the audience ask questions?

Will stationary audience mic on a stand be necessary?

Will the audience pass around a wireless mic?

If no audience mic, will the speaker repeat audience questions?
(if no audience mic, audience audio will be marginal)

Will PowerPoint be used? If so, can we get a copy before the event? (we will transfer the powerpoint slides to video and edit them into the presentation so they can be viewed clearly)

Will the presenter use any physical props or printed materials during the presentation?

Will there be any special lighting in the room (spotlights) in addition to fluorescent lighting?

Will the lights be very low to accommodate a power point projection?

Will the lighting change during the presentation (will room lights be turned off during powerpoint segments)?

How will the presentation played back (DVD player, YouTube, Vimeo?)

If the presentation will be broadcast on TV or cable, what digital file format does the broadcaster require? (for programs over 45 minutes, you may need to provide us with a hard drive to give the completed program to the broadcaster)

Are there any restrictions for camera placement? (Will it block audience view? Will it be far from the speaker? Will it be on a balcony?)

TV Commercial Production Checklist

A. Schedule/Prep
____ Bid sheet
____ Copy/Script
____ Storyboard
____ Prepro Mtg. Client
____ Prepro Mtg. Company
____ Casting Session
____ View Casting Tapes
____ Scout Date
____ Shoot Date
____ Music/Pre-records

B. Talent
____ Principals Booked
____ SAG Extras
____ Non-SAG Extras
____ SAG Waivers
____ Payroll Company
____ Contracts/Vouchers
____ W-4s
____ Station 12
____ Product Conflict
____ Schedule Conflict
____ Agents
____ Call Time/PU
____ Animals
____ Children
____ Stunts
____ Script

C. Travel
____ Train/Plane
____ Hotel
____ Taxi/Limo
____ Motorhome
____ Auto Rent
____ Truck Rent
____ Mileage Allow.
____ Secure Parking 24hr.
____ Cash
____ Other Vehicles

D. Legal
____ Personal Releases
____ Location Releases
____ Ins. Certificates

____ Time Cards
____ Invoices/Deal Memos

E. Studio/Location
____ Studio-MOS/Sound
____ Location Local/Distant
____ Weather Report/Tides
____ Sunrise/Sunset Times
____ Security Guard
____ Neighbors
____ Parking
____ Location Scout Form

F. Local Official Relations
____ Film Commission Contact
____ Local Govt. Contact
____ Police/Fire Contact
____ Film Permit
____ Merchant's Assoc.

G. Art/Props
____ Location(s)
____ Products/Color Corrects
____ Action Props
____ Set Dressing/Colors
____ Builds/Paint
____ Picture Vehicles
____ Greens
____ Special EFX
____ Food
____ Home Economist
____ Economist Supplies
____ Economist Transport
____ Agency/Client Items
____ Tabletop/Backgrounds
____ Car Cleaning Items

H. Stylist
____ Makeup
____ Wardrobe/Costumes
____ Mirrors
____ MU Table, Chairs, Lights
____ Wardrobe Rack
____ Changing Area
____ Iron/Board
____ Kits
____ Transport

I . Equipment

_____ Camera/Lens/Support
_____ Dollies
_____ Cranes
_____ Steadicam
_____ Special Mounts/Rigs
_____ Camera Car/Trailer
_____ Aircraft/Mount
_____ Camera Van
_____ Grip/Elec Pack/Truck
_____ Generator
_____ Minor Expendables
_____Slate
_____ Gels/Bulbs
_____ Sound Pack/PB
_____ Video Assist/PB
_____ TelePrompTer
_____ Shipment
_____ Special Light
_____ Video PB
_____ Video Assist Stock

J. Crew
_____ Crew Booking
_____ Transport
_____ Call Times
_____ Location/Studio
_____ Union Deal

K. Production Dept.
_____ First Aid Kit
_____ Fire Extinguisher
_____ Mats/Tarps/Kraft Paper
_____ Chairs/Tables
_____ Cleanup Stuff
_____ Furniture Pads
_____ Auto Service Tools
_____ Walkie-Talkies
_____ Cellular Phone
_____ Loud Hailer
_____ Foul Weather Gear

_____ Wet Work Gear
_____ Sun/Insect Protection
_____ Still Camera/Battery
_____ PC Envelopes
_____ PC Vouchers
_____ Blank POs Lab/Sound
_____ Postage Stamps
_____ Petty Cash
_____ Payphone/Parking Coins
_____ Cater/Bfast/Lunch/Dinner
_____ Craft Services
_____ Local Restaurants
_____ Telephone
_____ Comfort Facilities
_____ Shelter
_____ Parking
_____ Fax Rental
_____ Copier Rental
_____Technical Consultant

L. Lab/Post
_____ Capture Video
_____ Sound Transfer
_____ Narration Recording
_____ Sound Mix
_____ Pulls Edit
_____ String Out
_____Rough Edit
_____Final Edit
_____ Color Correction and Transitions
_____ Original Animation or Graphics
_____ Titles/Cards
_____ Animation/Archive
_____ Dubs
_____ Air/Delivery Date
_____ DVD copies
_____ Video files for broadcast, broadband and computer

MISC NOTES:

Standard Audio/Visual Appearance Release

I hereby grant to _____ and its licensees and assigns the right to use my name, likeness, image, and voice as recorded for the audio/visual program titled:

_____.

I understand that this program is intended for viewing by the general public, and may be exhibited to the general public throughout the world in perpetuity. Videocassettes, the Internet, DVDs, over-the-air broadcasting, cable, satellite, and all other audio/visual duplication and distribution methods may be used to distribute this program to the general public. Still photos of my image may be extracted from this program and may be used for promotional purposes.

I grant this right unconditionally, without expectation of any payment to me.

I represent that I am lawfully able to grant the rights described above:

_____

Name of person appearing in program (please print)

_____

Signature of person appearing in program or parent or legal guardian if above is under age 18:

_____   _____

Date   phone or email

Production Office Supplies/Equipment

2x4" spiral bound note pads

¾" masking tape

College-ruled 3-hole paper

Click Ballpoint pens

Highlighter

Sharpie

Mechanical Pencils

Measuring Tape

Paper clips

Rubber Band Assortment

Scissors

Stapler- Staples

Scotch Tape & Dispenser

Post-it Notes

Ruler/Straight Edge

Sharpie Marker

Tablet/Smartphone

Bad weather/environment gear (umbrella, boots, raincoat/poncho, hat, clothing layers)

Tool Kit-basics (screw drivers, pliers, wire cutter, hammer, adjustable wrench)

Swiss Army Knife

Sample Video Script

Sc#		VIDEO	AUDIO
1		Edgy text animation: "finally trendy and affordable are on the same side"	Urban Tech Music, VO: Finally, trendy and affordable are on the same side…
2		General montage	at CitiSide, "Charlotte's Best Kept Secret."
3		Multi-image collage animation	It's a new urban lifestyle, featuring the convenience of city living in a great-looking neighborhood that says welcome home!
4		Arena, stadium, restaurant, Theater, museum, entertainment poster	The bustle of uptown Charlotte with its pro sports, museums, restaurants and entertainment is just a few miles down the road.
5		NoDa	So is No-DA, Charlotte's blossoming arts district where you can catch a show, visit a gallery, and get a great meal.
6		Big Box stores	The shopping centers in University City are a quick five minutes away, with all the big popular stores you want and need.
7		Quiet street	It's close to jobs and shopping, but away from traffic. Living in CitiSide means less commuting time and more time for you!
8		Bi-Lo & shops	Next to CitiSide is a full-size supermarket, restaurants, and more right at your fingertips.
9		Pix of Afro-Am, Latin, Asian shops	Citiside homeowners enjoy the enticing international flavor of East Charlotte. You can explore dozens of unique shops, ethnic restaurants, and specialty grocers that will add spice to your lifestyle.
10		Hospital	A wide choice of medical facilities, urgent care centers, and the respected University Medical Center are close by.

Call Sheet

Production_____   **Date**_____

Location_____

Production Phone_____

Contact_____

POSITION	NAME	ok/c/NOTES/TIME
Director		
Producer		
AD		
DP		
AC		
Gaffer		
2nd Elec.		
Key Grip		
Grip		
Stylist		
Props		
Sets		
Sound		
Video Asst.		
PA		
Stills		

_____

_____

Location:

Caterer_____ #B_____ #L_____ #D_____

Times:_____

Caterer

notes:_____

Camera

Lights

Dolly

Genny

Lab

Video Asst.

Sets

Talent:

Transportation: Other:

Script Breakdown Sheet Sample

Breakdown Sheet # 1	SCRIPT BREAKDOWN SHEET "FILM TITLE"		Scene # 1

Int / Ext	Set: At daytime outside and inside a house	Day / Night	Pages
External and internal		Day- Lunchtime	
Description: Woman watching the original Mr. Postman song and then the Postman riding his bike delivers a letter.		Location	Studio
		Outside/inside a house	

Cast	Extra	Stunts
Jordan Adeyemi Genie Abbott	None	None

Props	Wardrobe	Vehicles
TV Hat Laptop Bag		Bicycle

Notes: Meet at the media suite at 1.00 o'clock and remember the props.

This is for Friday 8th October 2010

Sample Blank Production Budget

DOCUMENTARY BUDGET				Date:		
Title:						
Notes:						
For More Information Please Contact:						
Subtotals						
ADMINISTRATIVE				$ -		
CREW				$ -		
EQUIPMENT				$ -		
MARKETING				$ -		
POST-PRODUCTION				$ -		
SUPPLIES				$ -		
TRAVEL				$ -		
Subtotal				$ -		
Contingency	10%			$ -	$ -	
GRAND TOTAL				$ -		
	REQD	AMT	COST	UNIT	TOTAL	
ADMINISTRATIVE						
Office Rent & Utilities				mo	$ -	
Phone				mo	$ -	
Photocopies				flat	$ -	
Express Shipping				flat	$ -	
Postage				flat	$ -	
Office Supplies				flat	$ -	
Office Equipment				flat	$ -	
Insurance				flat	$ -	
Research				flat	$ -	
Pre-production				flat	$ -	
Misc.					$ -	
SUBTOTAL					$ -	
CREW/STAFF						
Executive Producer				wk	$ -	
Producer				wk	$ -	
Director				wk	$ -	
Writer				flat	$ -	
Camera/DP				day	$ -	
Audio				day	$ -	

Grip/PA					day	$	-	
Assoc. Producer					wk	$	-	
Misc.						$	-	
SUBTOTAL						$	-	
EQUIPMENT								
Camera Package					day	$	-	
Audio Package					day	$	-	
Camera Package					day	$	-	
Crane					day	$	-	
Helicopter					day	$	-	
Steadicam					day	$	-	
Walkie-Talkies					day	$	-	
Other						$	-	
SUBTOTAL						$	-	
MARKETING								
PR Coordinator					wk	$	-	
Press Kit Design					flat	$	-	
Press Kit Printing					flat	$	-	
Advertising					flat	$	-	
Postage					flat	$	-	
Screeners					flat	$	-	
Video Promo					flat	$	-	
Expendable Supplies					flat	$	-	
Misc.						$	-	
SUBTOTAL						$	-	
POST-PRODUCTION								
Logging					day	$	-	
Transcriptions					30 min.			
Edit System					day	$	-	
Animation					hr	$	-	
Misc. Graphics					hr	$	-	
Rostrum Photography					hr	$	-	
Archival Research					wk	$	-	
Archival License						$	-	
VO Talent					flat	$	-	
VO Recording					hr	$	-	
Sound Edit/Mix					hr	$	-	
Original Music					flat	$	-	
Music Licenses					flat	$	-	
DVD Authoring								
Subtotal						$	-	
SUPPLIES								
Recording Media					ea	$	-	
Batteries					flat	$	-	
Lighting Expendables					flat	$	-	

Blank DVDs							
Craft Services				flat	$	-	
Misc.					$	-	
Subtotal					$	-	
TRAVEL							
Pre-production				flat	$	-	
Airfares				ea	$	-	
Hotel				day	$	-	
Meals				day	$	-	
Excess Baggage				flat	$	-	
Auto Rental				flat	$	-	
Mileage/Gas				flat	$	-	
Truck Rental				flat	$	-	
Parking/Tolls				flat	$	-	
Misc.					$	-	
Subtotal					$	-	

Tips for Clear Broadcast Writing

1. Reduce number of words.
   a. John once said; NOT John at one time said
2. Reduce unnecessary adjectives.
   a. while thinking; NOT while quietly thinking.
3. Sentences should be subject, verb, object.
   a. I'm going to Charlotte; NOT the city I'm going to is Charlotte
4. Reduce prepositional phrases with possessives
   a. the boy's house; NOT the house of the boy
5. Don't use "that" word.
   a. they knew he would leave; NOT they knew that he would leave
6. Use active voice
   a. I think I will work there; NOT I am thinking I will work there
7. Use inverted pyramid style beginning with solid lead
   a. who, what, when, where, how: "President Lincoln was assassinated last night at Ford's Theater in Washington DC. An unknown assailant shot the president in the head, then escaped out a back door."
8. Control sprawl; use short sentences, avoid subordinate clauses
   a. NOT Jane, who was president, and spoke French without an accent, though she was from England, and graduated from college, was a nice person, when she felt good.
9. Ignore "folklore rules"
   a. It's OK to use contractions. And to begin sentences with "and"
10. Don't use meaningless words
    a. actually, really, certain, various, very, basically...
11. Don't use "in order to"
    a. to open the box, use a knife; NOT in order to open the box, use a knife
12. Don't begin a sentence with "there"
    a. Many people have lost money; NOT There are many people who have lost money
13. How to construct a story
    a. Collect facts (underline from other works, interviews, observation notes)
    b. List facts
    c. Group facts in Outline
    d. Fill in outline with connecting words to construct sentences
14. Don't needlessly capitalize.
    a. The teacher is from Baltimore, NOT the Teacher is from BALTIMORE.

15. Use good grammar, spelling, and punctuation.
    a. Use Word spell/grammar check
16. When listing things, limit examples to 2-3
17. Title and include byline and date for all written work
18. When saving a file, give it a good identifying file name like:
    maier_10.12.14newspromo_1

Sample Invoice

10101010

ACME VIDEO
PRODUCTIONS
203 Seagate Dr.
Cornelius, NC
28031
704-123-4567
info@acmeprod.com

TO   CLIENT NAME
CLIENT
ADDRESS
CLIENT CITY STATE ZIP
CLIENT PHONE NUMBER

DATE   16-Aug-11

FOR

TOTAL AMOUNT DUE   **$0.00**

Thank you!

Federal ID#   xxx-xx-xxxx

How to Get Your Name in the IMDb

- enjoy communicating with others
- give others a chance to speak and pay attention when they do
- be positive; make yes your most frequent answer
- be accountable; accept blame and don't give excuses
- accept criticism and advice—don't argue
- be honest, but not rude
- show respect for employers, co-workers, and audiences
- know your work is about the project, not about you
- know the difference between being persistent and being a pest
- have good time management; be punctual
- participate, react, respond, contribute
- be a self-starter
- be detail-oriented and organized
- complete your work
- don't leave your stuff around
- don't trust people who do not take notes, including yourself
- use proper grammar
- have professional dress, look, and demeanor
- be technology-friendly
- be flexible; stuff happens, things change, better ideas come along, people forget
- be curious—enjoy trying new things
- ask questions when you're stuck; but be sure you're stuck first
- back-up your work
- unhappy, un-paid students, interns and volunteers will not make happy paid employees; every successful person once worked and studied for "free," got insulted, got ignored, and got over it, before they got the job

Section 9

Advanced Essentials of Audio Production

Note: Study this section concurrently with **Section 5, Basic Audio for Video.** Section 5 has photos and illustrations of the concepts and products covered in this section. This section goes into greater depth regarding digital audio and multi-track recording than Section 5.

Characteristics of sound

- Sound occurs on the molecular level, when molecules bump against each other, and that bump is passed to another molecule; these slight movements are picked up as sounds by the ears, when the chain reaction of molecules eventually pushes against the eardrum.
    - Sound can be transferred through most substances; air, water, wood, metal, etc.
    - The denser the material, the more closely packed the molecules are, and the more efficient the transmission of sound.
    - Sound moves in waves; like tuning fork in water and measured by
    - Frequency is cycles per second, and heard as pitch (high note/low note)
        - Measured in cycles or hertz
    - Amplitude is loudness
        - Measured in decibels

- Energy transference creates distortions in original waves
    - Phase differences due to echo reinforcement and cancellations
    - Different substances affect sound movement, variations in transmission of frequencies and phase changes
    - Harmonics are multiples of the fundamental frequency
        - Create harmonies, which are usually pleasant, but can be boring if to regular
    - Overtones are sounds that fall between the harmonics
        - Create dissonances, which create tension, and resolve into harmonies and make music more interesting.
    - Timbre is the specific recognizable qualities of a sound
        - Distinguish a flute from a clarinet
    - Human hearing is 20 Hz to 20,000 Hz (vibrations)
        - Lower the number, lower the sound
        - Ranges are bass, mid-range, and treble
    - Sound can be recorded by mechanically capturing the impressions made by the energy of sound waves when they affect a physical material
        - Initial impression on a microphone, or electronic or physical transducer

Music basics

- Knowing even a little music theory is extremely important in recording engineering. The best way is studying an easy instrument like harmonica, flute, ukulele, or guitar. The cheapest is learning to sing. Any church choir will teach you for free. Start now, if you have never taken music lessons.
- Musical Notes
    - Individual sound with specific pitch
    - Each sound/note has a specific frequency measured in hertz;
    - Musical Scale
        - Western music since the 1600s has mainly used only 12 "tempered" notes in a scale that increase by a set band of frequencies.
        - Those 12 notes are one "octave."
        - Scales can have many octaves.
        - Each octave doubles the frequency of the preceding octave
        - Example with 440 Hz, 220 Hz is one octave down, 880 Hz is one octave up
            - Some instruments can hit many more than the 12 tempered notes (strings can be bent, horns and flutes can be varied)

- Melody, Harmony, and Dissonance
  - Melody is the tune
  - Harmony are harmonics/tones that multiply the melody line notes in an even division (example 20, 40, 60, etc.)
  - Dissonance or overtones are notes that do not evenly divide into the melody notes (example 17, 29, 43). They disrupt the sound waves resulting in cancellations.
    - Dissonance creates tension/conflict that is released by harmony, making music more interesting.
  - Major/Minor Keys
    - Major is happy sound
    - Minor is sad sound
    - They are often combined in songs to create conflict, and resolution which creates a musical narrative (tells a story- boy meets girl, boy loses girl, boy gets girl).
- Time/Pacing
  - Notes may sustain and can be held for several beats
  - Notes are played in a specific rhythm
  - Notes are played at a specific pace
  - Notes are played with different attack and decay times
  - Each of above create a mood
- Music and Mood
  - Music stimulates the brain in a positive way; scientists are studying why the brain works this way, and haven't found definitive answers.
    - Work goes faster
    - Time goes faster
    - Pain and stress are reduced
    - Imagination is assisted
  - Music assists telling a video story by enhancing mood and anticipating the storyline

Basic electronics for audio production

- Electricity Theory
  - Watts
    - Measurement of amount of electrical power
    - Watts= Volts x Amps
  - Alternating and Direct Current (AC/DC)
    - Electronics use Direct Current

- Batteries use Direct Current
- Alternating Current is "wall socket" electricity or "mains"

- The Audio Chain
  - Pick-up
    - Microphone
    - Instrument
    - Pre-amplifier- Increases signal power (wattage) to a level that is easily controlled by electrical processors
    - Converter-Converts analog signal to digital audio file
    - Recorder- Records digital audio files to memory (hard drive, memory cards)
    - Player-Plays back digital audio files
  - Effects Processor- Changes the sound of the original audio
  - Amplifier – increases audio volume for playback through loudspeakers or headphones
  - Monitor-Speakers, headphones and meters

- Balanced vs. Unbalanced Systems

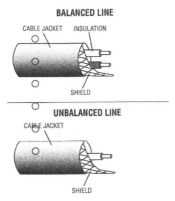

  - Long cables act as antennae and can pick up unwanted radio signals or other electronic noise
  - Balanced systems are grounded with a metal mesh or metal membrane surrounding the signal conducting cables.
  - The ground connection eliminates electrical noise like radio or other ambient electronic or electrical waves that may enter the cable
  - Unbalanced systems are cheaper and used for home electronics

- Connections **(see cable and connectors poster at end of book)**
  - Cable types

- Gender
- Shielding
  - Most common connectors
    - RCA
      - Home/semi-pro
    - XLR
      - Locking
      - Balanced cable with grounded shield
    - Phone/TRS (tip, ring, sleeve)
      - ¼"
      - Mini 1/8"
- Line level or Mic level
  - Power of signal input
  - Determines amount of pre-amplification
  - Generally a switch, but sometimes variable
  - Line level is amplified and not subject as much to radio wave interference
- Amplification and gain
  - Controls loudness by electronically increasing the power (wattage) of the signal
  - Distortion
    - Volume is so loud that amplifier cannot process it and creates white noise and chaotic wave forms
    - Clipping, Over-modulation mean same thing
- Audio playback channels
  - Generally stereo (2 channels-left and right)
  - Surround sound has 5-8 channels, sometimes more
  - Each channel has its own signal; when all channels played back, creates a wider special audio environment
  - Multi-track recording
    - In production many channels are used to create a more complex audio production with multiple sounds (instruments, effects, vocal) that are mixed into the final playback channels
  - Multi-channel playback
    - Stereo is most common e.g. headphones and speakers
    - Mono is less dynamic and used mostly in cell phones and PA systems (stadiums, shopping malls)

- 5.1 and above used in theaters for films where people are stationary to create dramatic environment
- Electronic noise is
  - Interference
  - Hardware malfunction
  - Digitization errors
  - Poor connections

Microphones

Types of microphones (see section 5 for images and more info)

- Dynamic
  - Sturdy
  - Do not require power outside of pre-amp
  - Least sensitive because require purely mechanical operation, no amplification in the mic
- Condenser
  - Require 48v phantom from mixer or battery powered pre-amp attached between mic and mixer
  - More sensitive and complex
  - More faithful sound capture due to sensitivity
  - Have more directionality
- Special design
  - Lavalier
    - Wearable body mic
    - Usually omni-directional so when talent turns head, stays within broad pickup pattern
  - PZM
    - Sensitive to wide field—used on round tables
  - Direct input musical instrument
    - Mounted on or inside instruments
  - Shotgun
    - Long mic, most directional
  - Stereo
    - Two mics with separate outputs in one housing
  - Headset mics
    - Ideal for sports and noisy news coverage
    - Include earphones

Microphone Design

- o Diaphragm
  - ▪ Vibrates mirroring sound waves
- o Transducer
  - o Converts movement of diaphragm to electrical current in same pattern as diaphragm movement
- • Pick-up patterns
  - o Omni-directional – picks up sound from all directions; no rejection
  - o Bi-directional - picks up sound from 2 directions 180 degrees apart only
  - o Cardiod – picks up sound in heart-shaped pattern
  - o Super cardiod - picks up sound in elongated heart shaped pattern
  - o Hyper-cardioid – picks up sound in nearly cigar shaped pattern
  - o Multi-directional – switchable pick-up patterns
- • On-mic switches (not all mics have all switches)
  - o On-off switch
  - o Bass Roll-off-proximity effect, ambient rumble
  - o Pick-up Pattern

Mic Problems

- • Feedback
- • Wind noise from mouth or excessive ambient air movement
- • Phasing (two or more mics cancelling each other)
- • Electrical fields (generate hums and buzzes)
- • Bad connections (clicks or buzzes)
- • Dead battery (condenser mics only)
- • Loose cable connections
  - o Cables make noise when jiggled
    - ▪ Taping connectors reduces connector noise
  - o Handle cables with care, they are fragile
  - o Bad cable connections are the #1 noise source
- • Physical damage to diaphragm/transducers
  - o Mics are fragile
  - o Need carrying cases
  - o Wind or voice plosives (p,b sounds) can damage diaphragms

- o Moisture can damage electronics or diaphragm when high humidity or abrupt temperature change
- o Dust can collect on diaphragm and damage or affect pickup quality

Speaking into a Mic

- 6 inches from mic is best
- Know what is the front of the mic and speak directly into it, not sides
- Plosives ("p" "s" "t" "b" "f") cause overload because of air coming from the mouth
- Proximity effect—heavily boosted base when too close to mic
- Sibilance- "S" sound creates distortion because it includes all frequencies and creates high sound energy
- Mics subject to hand noise, hold firm and still
- Speakers do not touch any mic directly when speaking, unless specifically designed for hand-holding

Mic Accessories

- Wind screens
    - o Internal
    - o External
        - ▪ Foam
        - ▪ Spit screen
        - ▪ Wind muff
- Shock mounts
    - o Isolate the microphone from handling noise on the mic body or transmitted up the connecting cable or mic stand
    - o Use a variety of elastic materials that absorb vibrations and prevent them from being transmitted to mic capsule
    - o Internal (handheld RE-50)- insulates the mic capsule from the mic body
    - o External (isolates mic from stand)
    - o Connecting cables should not be tightly stretched
- Mic stands
    - o Floor
    - o Booms
    - o Desk

Digital Production

Digital Audio Theory

Analog audio is sampled by an electronic converter that creates electrical pulses into digital code.

- The processor samples electromagnetic representation to create slightly imperfect, but consistent analog illusion
  - Much like video frame rate – persistence of hearing
  - 44.1kh is most common sample rate – means sampling of waveform is done 44,100 times per second.
  - Quantizing converts analog to digital numbers; each number represents a part of a sound;
  - 16 bit is normal CD bit depth—each bit is a piece of data (amplitude or frequency taken in a sample, so in one second 44,100 x 16 or 705,600 measurements are recorded; greater bit depths of 24, 32, 64 are available but only used in production, not distribution
  - Samples are discrete packets of code in digital streams that are stored in files (.mp3, .wav)
  - No audio degradation in reproduction, because perfect, individual numbers are being reproduced, not imperfect mechanical copies
  - Files can be edited precisely, because code is being edited bit by bit
    - Small computers suitable
    - Various software available: Audition, Sound Forge, Cakewalk, Logic, Nuendo, Ableton, cuBase, ProTools, and many cheap imitators.
  - Advantages of digital
    - Basically no noise or mechanical artifacts (wow, flutter, hiss, rumble, print-through, phasing, additional spurious overtones, clipping) in multiple generations, as is the case with old analog styles of vinyl records or magnetic tape.
    - Requires less storage space
    - Machines are smaller; no motors, no transports low voltage requirements

- Uses less electric power; smaller motors, fans, low voltage
- Non-destructive editing
- File types
  - There are many types of audio files.
  - The larger the file, the higher the quality
  - File types include: .wma, .mp3, .aiff, etc.
  - File types compress the audio samples based on mathematical compression schemes that create audio for specific hardware-dependent situations
  - Files for phone playback only can be much smaller than files of original recordings
  - Different file types give the advantage of tailoring a specific type and size to a specific purpose. For example files that need to be transmitted by cell-phone travel faster if they're smaller; same as with Internet transmission; CD playback, DVD playback; hard drive playback; the better the audio quality, the larger the file size.
  - Original recordings should be made with the highest quality audio file type
  - The final project will be "rendered" to the appropriate file type by compression calculations considering sampling rates and bit depth.

Digital Audio Editing

Overview of Digital Audio Production Software

- Capabilities
  - Single and multi-track
    - Recording
    - Processing
    - Mixing
    - Mastering
- Workflow
  - Create audio File
  - Edit audio file
  - Apply effects
  - Mix all tracks

- o Bounce/render audio to final playable version (mono, stereo, or more for video)
- Window layout/workspace/docking
  - o Workspace flexible via docking windows and include
    - Toolbar
    - Status bar
    - Timeline
    - Media file library
  - o Pull-down or hover menus used to accomplish tasks
  - o Navigation
    - Keyboard shortcuts
    - Scroll bars
    - Cursor controls
      - Time selection
      - Audio scrub
    - Transport panel
      - Play and Loop
  - o Metering
    - Several metering options selectable
- Set-up
  - o Project settings
  - o Preferences settings
  - o Use two drives for best results (program and media)
- Recording audio files
  - o Recording in multi-view, track must be armed
- Importing audio files/CD ripping
  - o Some production software can import and convert files directly from commercial CDs (.cda files)
- Playing back audio files
- Editing audio files
  - o Selecting audio
  - o Copying, cutting, pasting, deleting
- Volume/amplitude adjustments
  - o Digital gain stages
    - Analog pre-amp
    - EFX-inserts
    - EFX-inserts processor
    - EFX inserts outs
    - Channel fader

- ▪ Master fader
- ▪ Mixdown normalizer
- Fades/dissolves
  - o Single and multi-track choices
- Envelopes
  - o Volume
  - o Pan
- Effects
  - o Incorporated into program
  - o Software plug-ins
  - o VST
- Arranging clips
  - o Creating work tracks
  - o Using multiple tracks for narration/interviews
  - o Cutting clips (Ctl+k)
  - o Extending & shortening tracks in multi-track view
- Moving clips
  - o Group and un-group
- Mixdown
  - o Choice of file types
- Burning to disc
  - o Audio files (.cda)- CD players only
  - o Data files (.mp3, .wav., .wma) computer players only, with a few exceptions

Mixing and Processing Audio

The Mixing Board

- Routing
  - o Routing selects which inputs go to which output
- Inputs
  - ▪ Mic level
  - ▪ Line level
- Sends and inserts
  - ▪ Monitor
  - ▪ Insert to effects out/in
  - ▪ Aux sends/returns
- Group

- Selects which output is used
  - Mix output
  - Speaker
  - Headphone
- Other common board controls
  - Cue
  - Solo
  - Talkback
  - Tone generator
  - Channel fader
  - Sub-master and master faders

Input Channel Strip Controls
- Volume fader
- Input gain/trim
- Input connector
- Phantom power
- EQ controls
  - Multi-band
  - Parametric
  - Band-pass/roll-off filters
- Stereo pan pot
- Level meters
- Pads
- PFL/AFL monitor switch
- Solo switch
- On-board effects channels
- Channel on/off switch
- Meters
  - Input
  - Output
  - VU meters-average level
- May include a peak-warning LED

Signal Processors

Digital processing features a nearly infinite variety of effects that can be added to recording, giving it enhanced interest due to increased complexity and individuality of a sound. Principal types of processing:

- Volume
  - Adjusts amplitude/loudness; which is the level of audio power
  - Simplest adjustment; lowers or raises all frequencies in an audio signal equally
  - Digital editors can lower or raise selected sections of an audio track

- Equalization (EQ)
  - Graphic
    - Fixed bandwidth for numerous frequency ranges with amplitude control only on a fixed bandwidth
    - Can have 3-32 fixed bands, generally
    - Adjustment by vertical slider with scale on left
    - Fixed band
    - Like a car stereo with hi-med-low settings, usually simple rotary knob
  - Parametric
    - Adjustable band width and adjustable amplitude "Q" control
    - Usually 3 ranges, but sometimes more
  - Filters
    - Band- controls large number of frequencies
    - Notch- controls small number of frequencies
- Compression/Limiting/Gating
  - Compressor- smooth automatic level control based on variable ratios
  - Limiter- fixed maximum volume level
  - Gate- automatically mutes signal when it falls below a certain threshold to eliminate noise in track.
  - Expander- same as gate
  - Normalizer- sets maximum volume level
  - De-esser- eliminates **sibilance**- distorted "s"

- Echo/Reverb
  - Adds attractive depth and dimension to audio replacing live sound quality lost in the recording studio
  - Mimics rooms with hard walls
  - Echo usually means a distinct echo (slap echo)

- Echo is a repeated sound – "hello, hello, hello"
  - Reverberation is a softer edged indistinct echo found in most live room situations.

- Chorus/ Phase Shift
  - Chorus is a close repetition of a sound immediately following the initial sound; like a slightly out-of-sync vocal chorus that makes a track sound richer, because it gives the illusion of more performers.
  - Phase shift (phasing or flanging) is an electronic effect that sounds like whooshing.

- Special EFX
  - See Adobe Audition/Pro Tools list of efx native to software package.
  - Add-in efx software available; extra purchase

- Multiple Effects Processor
  - Software package
    - Includes hundreds of pre-sets and adjustable parameters
  - Hardware
    - Often in electronic music instruments/amps for live performance

- Voice processors
  - EQ ,compression/limiting/gating, and d-essing controls especially for voice range correction and enhancement

- VST instruments
  - Virtual Studio Technology – plug-ins
  - Software-created musical instruments, sounds, samplers, and processors
  - Hundreds of brands and styles used for professional recording.

Recorders/Media

Compact Disc (CD)

- CDs standard in Music/Radio Playback
- Have their own file format (.cda) that can only be played back in CD players from a CD
- Being replaced by flash drives
- Excellent digital quality
- Broadcast facilities have two units one for play, one for cue
- Broadcast players
  - More heavy duty durable
  - Cue wheel for precise location
  - Easy individual track ID and selection
  - Large countdown LED readout for timing
  - CD cart players protect the CD and allow selection playing of two tracks back-to-back from same CD
- Multi-play CD players "jukebox" can hold 300 CDs
- Higher audio quality than MP3 or other highly compressed digital formats
- CD Tips:
  - Store music as 16 bit digital words (samples) 44,100 times per second
  - 650 Mb storage on a CD
  - 74-80 min music play time
  - Handle on edge or center
  - Recorded from center out
  - Clean with soft cloth in out straight, not circular motion, some chemical cleaners (alcohol) used for really dirty
  - Dirt and scratches will make CDs skip or become totally unplayable
  - Adhesive labels or crayon-like or wet-ink markers can damage players; never use. Mark with fast-drying permanent markers
  - All computers include CD Recorders in the optical drive

Flash RAM or Hard Disc Recorders

- Silicon chip memory
  - Can vary compression for higher quality
  - Internal removable memory cards

- Very small
- Very fast
- Can hold hours of audio; good for very small, light, portable recorders

- SB Flash drives
  - Cheap, very small and easy and work in all computers with USB ports (every computer for past 7-8 years includes USB)
  - Can be slower than hard drives
  - Limited size compared to hard drives, but capacity increasing rapidly, nearly doubling every year. Currently 32 Gb becoming common.

- Hard drives
  - Come in many versions from large studio servers to portables the size of a coin
  - i-pod is example of very small hard drive
  - Huge memory capacity
- Digital memory recorders/players
  - Computer-based or micro computers
  - Many portable models of varying mechanical quality
  - Audio quality pretty much the same
- Legacy analog media
  - Vinyl records making comeback for purer "analog" sound
  - 1/8" Audiocassettes have distinctive analog sound that may not be highest quality, but attractive because "old school."

Audio Chain/Studio Layout

Input Equipment Overview

- CD player
- Computer
- Legacy (tape, optical, vinyl records,)
- Microphones
- Network
  - Intranet
  - Satellite
  - Internet
  - Telephone
  - Sub-mixer

- Mixing Board/Panel/Desk
  - Analog
    - Some prefer because all controls on all channels visible
    - Good ones can be very expensive because mechanical elements must be highest quality
  - Digital
    - Some prefer because greater number of tracks and efx controls available in smaller, space, therefore less expensive
  - Hybrid analog/digital boards gaining popularity
- Processing Equipment
  - EQ – tone control
  - EFX- dozens of digital efx that allow adjustment of sound waves in unlimited variety
  - Compressors
  - Limiters
  - Filters
  - Voice processors (combine all of above)

Output Equipment Overview

- Monitors
  - Speakers
  - Headphones
  - Electronic scopes
- Recorders or Transmitter
  - Computers
  - Radio and TV transmitter
  - Internet streamer
  - Disc burner (CD and DVD)

Studio Layout

- Furniture/Atmosphere
  - Aesthetics
    - Attractive, professional setting helps creativity lower stress working environment
    - Makes better webshot
    - Muted colors/natural wood usually preferred
    - Artwork can be used

- Impresses tours/investors/sponsors
  - Custom work surfaces
  - Rack mount
  - Lighting
  - Ergonomic considerations
    - Chair
    - Height
    - Accessibility to equipment
    - Visibility
- Sound Considerations
  - Diffusion/absorption treatments on walls
    - Wall panels
      - Sometimes adjustable area to liven space
      - Fiberglass panels
      - Foam panels
      - Draperies to convert easily to livelier space
  - Carpets on floor
    - Sometimes moveable rugs to reveal resonant wooden floors for a livelier space
  - Room tone/machine noise isolated
    - Computer should have isolation cabinets
      - Must have quiet air or water cooling
    - Sound isolation/soundproofing
      - Walls
        - Fiber Glass insulation between stud walls
        - 6" studs
        - Double layer of sheet rock laid horizontal and vertical
        - High lead content doors
        - Door gaskets
      - Glass
        - Double or triple layer glass
        - Glass mounted at downward slanting angle
      - Diffusion
        - Wall panels
          - Fiberglass panels

- Foam panels
- Draperies
- Quilted moving blankets
    - Need to consider noisy nearby environment and avoid
        - Airports
        - Factories
        - Highways
        - Construction sites
        - Elevator noise
        - Plumbing noise
        - Crowds
        - Noisy weather (thunderstorms, hail, rain patter on roof)
        - Air handling
            - Need good air conditioning that is also very quiet
                - Accomplished by sound treating air ducts with insulation and baffles
- Music recording studios
    - Heavily sound proofed and sound treatment
    - Generally smaller than before, because most recording is done with multi-tracking and overdubbing; recording one track at a time, so room doesn't have to fit dozens of musicians.
    - Many larger instruments like pianos and drum kits are digital in many studios, so don't need much space
    - Usually larger mixing console with more controls, channels

Music Recording Studio Basics

Overview

- The recording studio layout and equipment
    - Analog outboard gear
    - Patch panel
    - Computer
    - Mixing board
    - Pre-amp rack
    - Monitor speakers-controller

- - Headphone mult box – enables connection of several headsets
  - Multi-track audio cards have several styles
    - USB and Fire wire connections
    - PCI card
      - Uses PCI card breakout box
  - Sound treatment/proofing
- Multi-track recording with Pro Tools 8-11
- Microphone techniques, placement, accessories
- Direct-in technique
- Recording
- Monitoring
- Overdubbing
- Processing
  - EQ
  - Reverb/echo
  - Compression/limiting
  - Special efx
- Mixing
  - Automation is control of all mixing functions by pre-programmed commands

Live Sound Topics

- Music concert sound reinforcement/event PA systems
  - Monitor- for performers
  - Front of House- for audience
- Permanent location PA systems
  - Analog mixing board
  - Inputs/outputs
  - Outboard processing equipment – EQ, Compressor, Gates, Echo
- Microphones
  - Wireless and Wired
  - Worn and Mounted
- Theater Production
  - Wireless mics
  - Playback cues
  - Front-of-house

- Monitor system
- Intercom system

Radio

Broadcast Audio Delay

- Records live program by several seconds (7-10) to allow producer to cut inappropriate language, etc. before it leaves the radio studio. A button must be pushed to activate it, and the station mutes for those few seconds, or a live sound effect is played to fill the muted space.
- Sneeze button enables announcer to momentarily cut mic to hide sneeze or other unwanted momentary sound.

Section 10 Audio Essential Lists

Protools Cheat Sheet

F2	Slip mode
F6	Trimmer Tool
F7	Selector Tool
F8	Grabber Tool
F10	Pencil Tool
Alt+	
A	View Entire Session
Numeric Keypad	
1	Rewind
2	Fast Forward
3	Record
4	Loop Playback
0	Play/Stop
Edit Navigation	
Go to Song Start	Start+Enter
Move curser to next region	Tab
Move cursor to previous region	Shift+Tab
Spacebar	Stop Start
Enter (keyboard)	Go to beginning of timeline
Enter (keypad)	Insert marker at cursor in marker bar
Group Regions	Ctl+Alt+G
Ungroup Regions	Ctl+Alt+U
1-5 keyboard	Zoom in pre-sets
F1	Shuffle
F2	Slip
F12	Enable record-punch-in
Ctl+	
C	Copy
E	Cut/split/edit
F	Fade
G	Group
Q	Center cut in screen
S	Save session
V	Paste
X	Cut
Y	Re-do
Z	Undo
2 (number keyboard)	View session properties
Windows Start Key +	
E	Zoom Toggle
R	Zoom-Out Horizontal
T	Zoom-In Horizontal
H	Undo Cut (Heal)
Mouse	
Alt+Scroll	Zoom-In-Out Horizontal Through Regions
Shft+Scroll	Scroll Horizontal Down Timeline
Alt+Shift+Scroll	Change Waveform Height
Double-click left	Select region
Triple –click left	Select track
Right click	View Menu

Left click drag	Select section
Left click	Place cursor/start mark

Protools Essential Operations

1. Set up session- disk management
2. Import audio
3. Add track
4. Set source in and signal out paths
5. Add audio file to track
6. Record audio to track
7. Cut audio
8. Fade audio head and tail
9. Crossfade audio regions in same track
10. Group/Ungroup Audio Regions
11. Group/Ungroup Audio Tracks
12. Shuffle edit
13. Edit –Mix views select
14. Automation (Volume & Pan) controls
15. Add Inserts for Effects
16. Add Sends for Monitoring
17. Add Busses for Grouping Efx
18. Add Groups for easier level control
19. Add Markers

Protools Essential Tips and Memory Joggers

1. Preferences
   a. Turn on Colors
   b. Backup every 2 minutes for 10 times
   c. Undo levels=20 to save on RAM
   d. New Session set 44.1 khz and 16 bit .wav files ***Our Studio Standard***
2. Playback Stutter
   a. If you have playback stutter, it may be your external hard drive. To fix, transfer session folder and all files to workstation desktop using "save copy as" command; when finished with session, "save copy " back to external drive and be sure to check-include all audio files.
   b. After transferring files from external drive to workstation desktop, unplug external drive from system before starting session from desktop.
   c. Be sure session properties match.
3. Playback Distortion
   a. Setup>Playback Engine> H/W Buffer Size (set to 1024); Host Processor (set to Max); un-check "minimize I/O latency"
4. Top Menu Bar
   a. Right click on title bar for title bar menu view
   b. Time line menu regions
      i. Top left- Choose SLIP edit mode
         1. Shuffle mode snaps when region is cut- this can cause trouble
      ii. Audio Zoom-in controls – Ignore; use mouse shortcut instead
      iii. Cursor tool select controls– use **super tool** (buttons 234 group)
      iv. Pencil Tool only used to draw on/adjust wave forms or controls (advanced)
      v. 1-5 button controls- zoom presets

      vi. Misc. command buttons
- 1. Zoom (single zoom in)
- 2. Tab to transients
- 3. Mirrored midi editing (advanced)
- 4. Linking Time Line and Edit Selection- Click to enable
- 5. Link Track and Edit Selection-Click to enable
- 6. Insertion follows playback switch- Click to enable
  - a. If selected(blue), cursor starts where it last stops
  - b. If unselected (grey), cursor returns to beginning of selection or Play Start Marker (blue arrowhead)

      vii. Transport controls – as marked
- 1. Loop- right click on Play button
- 2. Record choices- (punch-in, etc.)right click on Record button

      viii. Rulers
- 1. Change by right click in Ruler header
- 2. Use only Min-Secs and Markers Rulers

5. TRACKS list
   a. Down arrow selects views
   b. Drag right edge to expand width to see more information
6. Regions List
   a. Shows each audio file
   b. Expanded view shows full disc address

7. Timeline
   a. Views
      i. Select mix or edit, or both in separate windows with cascade
      ii. Wave form height adjustment in track: first right column waveform icon
   b. Tool Bars
      i. Use Super tool
      ii. Set counter format using down arrow in window
      iii. Edit mainly in Slip; Shuffle to close gaps; avoid Grid and Spot
   c. Track information section
      i. Down arrow top left selects views
      ii. Sample or tick display button
      iii. Track title box
      iv. Track Record Enable (red with white dot)
      v. Solo Switch (S)
      vi. Mute Switch (M)
      vii. Track view selector box
      viii. Automation-volume, pan, mute
   d. Inserts/Sends columns
      i. Add plug-in effects
      ii. Routing input signals
   e. I/O button
      i. Select track inputs (preamps), outputs (record channels), and sends
   f. Right click on track for track menu view
   g. Region is an event/cut/scene on a track
   h. Track is a group of events/regions controlled by a fader
      i. ProTools treats stereo as two individual tracks
   i. Fades
      i. If fade icon doesn't appear, delete fades (right click>delete fades)
      ii. Be sure auto fade on cut preference is not set
      iii. Crossfades - click on fade icon at bottom of track where regions meet and drag across timeline

    j.   Importing audio
        i. Always convert audio to be sure the file is in session folder
    k.   Moving and Selecting
        i. To drag cursor along time line, select Options>Dynamic Transport
        ii. Blue arrowhead moves cursor start mark
        iii. "Link timeline to edit" on preference to always show selector cursor on track
        iv. Blue up and down arrows are selection markers on time scale
        v. Gold vertical line/dot marker are selection markers for selected track
        vi. Scrolling Timeline Choices: Options>Page or Continuous
        vii. Selecting (left click> drag) time scale selects a section
        viii. Shift+left click selects multiple regions, enabling moving all
        ix. Shift copies cursor on multiple tracks
        x. Selecting (left click drag) track selects track
        xi. Shuttle button removes gap and snaps regions
        xii. Slip allows dragging clips anywhere
        xiii. Grouping-Shift +left click
        xiv. To move a group, move longest track first
    l.   Edit sequence
        i. Enter to move to beginning of track
        ii. Trim in Slip Mode
        iii. Select to group and move all regions to right of trimmed area (shift, grab, left click at end); go to Shuffle mode; grab first region and drag to tall of preceding clip
    m.   Automation of volume, pan, mute
        i. Automation Track Activation: Window>Automation> Suspend or un-suspend button.
        ii. View automation track click down arrow
        iii. Make automation points only when pencil tool is selected
        iv. Delete all automation by selecting automation lane and "del"
    n.   Click track Adjustment is under Setup
    o.   Master fader track is not automatic, must be added in "new track" window.
    p.   A-Z Button/ Keyboard Focus enables Keyboard key only commands
    q.   .ptf is a Protools session file- does not contain audio!
    r.   Always use auto input monitoring

8. Effects/Processing
    a.   Click Presets as starting point
    b.   To save your customized settings as preset: click down arrow in Preset button and "Save Settings As" with name and date to ID
    c.   Elastic Audio and Elastic Pitch not very helpful for general use. Other plug-ins do better job.

9. Mixing
    a.   Metering Post Fader- Options>PreFader Metering (uncheck to meter your mix out level, not input)

MISCELLANEOUS TIPS

- If working in PT 9-11, you can save your session as a previous version: File>Save Copy In...>Session Format>(select choice from down menu). This must be done to work on computers with PT 8.

Random Notes

- Protools' record modes changed through clicking the **Transport Record** button

- Playlist allows adding new recordings on the same track by adding "sub tracks" so you can easily compare various takes—click down arrow next to Track Name
- Leave Input Monitor selected except **when auto punching-in; use auto input monitoring**
- Group command selects all desired tracks—good for drums or other multi-mic controls, so that all processing given to one track is performed on the entire group
- Stereo files are imported as 2 mono files in separate tracks.
- Use EFX Buses to reduce processing power required when using the same effect over a range of tracks, like eq, verb, and compression.
- Find Disc Allocation under Set-up to select where your files are saved
- Keyboard Focus mode (Yellow/Black box on left corner of timeline) allows plain letter keyboard controls (no alt, ctl, or shift required)
- To Fade In/Out track, hover cursor in the upper left or right corner to reveal FI/F/O icon.
- Click Menu Bar to activate hover tips
- Hold down Start key to turn on audio scrubber while scrubbing
- Use Broadcast .wav file, because it records time code in audio file which helps in re-constructing sync.

Setting Up Protools Control A

Set I/O for each session
- **Set-Up>I/O>Import Settings> gaston normal 01> OK**

Monitor Station- Studio and Control Room
- **To monitor Playback and Talkback in Studio: Cue Source set to ST1**
- **To monitor Talkback only in Studio: Cue Source set to AUX**

HUI Setup for Mackie Universal Pro Controller
1. Set-up>Peripherals>Midi Controllers
   #1 HUI   MidiIn2   MidiOUT2   #8
   #2 HUI   MCUPro USB in   MCUPro USB out
   (above is correct when extender is left of the master)
2. Also check Setup>MIDI>Input Devices>Check all Boxes
3. To set up HUI on MCU, shut down, then re-start holding down "select" buttons on ch1&2 on main and extender. Select HUI by pressing multi black knob

Furman Mix Station
- Motu 3,4,5,6 out patched to Furman 1,2,3,4
- Stereo LR control currently inactive.

Setting Headphone Monitor Mix in Pro Tools
- View Send buss A-E in Mix window
- Select Outputs Furman 1, Furman 2, Furman 3, Furman 4
- View expanded send with fader and meter
  - View>Expanded Sends>Select Send A
- Set to Pre-Fader in pop-up send fader
- Adjust levels in pop-up send fader

To activate Focusrite channels 9-16 Set sample rate 44.1; Clock Source to Internal

To record instrument Direct Input in Control Room
- **Use Input 17 and/or 18, set to <u>line level</u>**

To record an instrument track in ProTools-
- Instrument track output to bus 1
- Audio Track input to bus 1

Access MOTU Cue Mix Internal mixer from task bar

MOTU to Octopre Connection Set-up
- Rear connections
  - Motu wordclock OUT BNC to Focusrite 1 (8-16) wordclock IN
  - Focusrite 8/16 wordclock out to Focusrite Wordclock 17-24 in
  - ADAT optical cables connect both Focusrites to Motu
- Front Connections
  - Set clock to Internal & Sample to 44.1

GAIN STAGES YOU MUST MONITOR !

Preamp input trim knob
Multi-preamp Main Out Master knob
Pro Tools track Playback/monitor levels
Pro Tools Effect input and output gain
Monitor Station Speaker level input knob
Monitor Station Master Volume knob
Speaker volume control knob

Adobe Audition Hot Tips & Cheat Sheet

1. Audition projects should be saved on an external hard disc drive;
2. USB flash drives run slow, and have limited capacity; more complex projects can crash them. If you absolutely need to use a flash drive, copy your data to the workstation desktop to work on your project, then save it back to the flash drive. This also gives you an automatic backup.
3. Do not edit your original file, edit a copy.
4. Do fine editing in multi-track view, not edit view-, or bounce between views.
5. Expand track heights in multi-track view for easier audio wave form editing.
6. Organize your files into project folders. Save all files to the correct folder. Specifically name folders including your last name and project number.
7. Specifically name all files for easy identification, and store them in the right folder.
8. **When saving a session check "Save All Associated Files" box to save all elements in session.**
9. Save audio files as .wav for best quality
10. Record all spoken voice tracks in mono (File>New>Channels>Mono)
11. View shortcut toolbars View>Shortcut Bar
12. ALWAYS monitor *recording* with headphones, to hear hidden problems
13. To monitor all tracks when overdubbing: Multitrack View>Session Properties>select Audition Mix; then select **Always Input**
14. Use two hands to edit- one on mouse, one on keyboard—much faster.

Multi-track view keyboard shortcuts

1. Turn on Meters **F10**
2. Hybrid Tool **R**　　**(select - left mouse hold; move - right mouse hold)**
3. Move/Copy Tool **V (left mouse hold; move clip)**
4. Time Select Tool **S (left mouse hold; selects area)**
5. Scrub Tool **A (left mouse hold; moves cursor variable speed)**
6. Multi-track view **9**　　Edit view **8 or** Toggle between views **F12**
7. Split clip (make a cut) **Ctl+K**
8. Zoom into timeline **+(plus)** zoom out **– (minus)**
9. Ripple delete **Alt+Del**
10. Keyboard shortcut list **Alt+k**
11. Clear volume points **Ctl+Del**
12. Group clips **Ctl+G;** ungroup clips **Ctl+U**
13. Cursor to timeline start **Home ;** Cursor to end of timeline **End**
14. Pause play **Shft+Ctl+Space**
15. Undo **Ctl+Z**
16. Re-do **Ctl+Y**
17. Cut selection **Ctl+X**
18. Copy selection **Ctl+C**
19. Paste selection **Ctl+V**
20. Record/Stop Toggle **Ctl + Spacebar**

Essential Audio Terms

Basic Science

1. Sound – acoustic energy that travels by vibrating molecules in set patterns of compression and rarefaction (expansion)
2. Wave (Sound wave)- a single compression and rarefaction of molecules that results in the perception of sound on the ear; generally sound consists of many waves that combine to create a specific recognizable signal.
3. Cycle- a single compression of molecules; the greater number of cycles, the higher the pitch/frequency
4. Amplitude-volume, loudness, or power of a sound
5. Attenuate- Reduce, or lower (as in attenuate (lower) the volume)
6. Frequency- number of cycles in a sound wave identified as a specific tone (do, re, me fa, so, la...)
7. Band- a range of frequencies in consecutive numerical order (20hz-100hz, 1,000hz-7,000hz) usually measured from low to high.
8. Treble- a range of high frequencies
9. Mid- a range of frequencies between high and low
10. Bass- a range of low frequencies
11. Resonate- to vibrate, creating and/or conducting sounds through air or solids, usually enhancing and coloring the original sound vibration
12. Fundamental- the original, pure single frequency (e.g. 100 Hz, 440 Hz, etc.) (very rare in nature)
13. Harmonic- additional frequencies created by the vibrating material that are even multiples of the fundamental (e.g. 200, 880); they result in pleasant "harmony"
14. Overtone- additional frequencies that fall between the harmonic frequencies
15. Timbre- The combinations of fundamentals, harmonics, and overtones that create a distinct sound for the audio source (e.g. voice, guitar, flute, drum)
16. Hertz- the unit of measurement of frequency (e.g. 100 Hz or 20,000hz) of a periodic event (cycles)

17. Pitch- the specific frequency of a specific sound measured in hertz, generally corresponding to the notes in a musical scale (do, re, me fa, so, la, ti, do)

18. Decibel (dB)- measurement of the level/amplitude/volume/power of a sound

19. Dynamic Range- The range of volume from lowest to highest level

20. Resonant Frequency- The frequency(ies) boosted due to the dimensions of an enclosed space that match certain wavelengths.

21. Frequency Response- The range of frequencies able to be accurately recorded or played back by audio equipment

22. Phase – sound wave synchronization that affects reinforcement or cancellation of frequencies depending on if they are in-phase or out-of-phase

Microphones

23. Microphone – Device used to pick-up live analog sound and convert it to electrical impulses

24. Dynamic Microphone – Sturdy microphone that does not use internal pre-amp or electronic power supply

25. Diaphragm- Thin membrane in mic that vibrates in reaction to live audio and is converted to an electrical signal.

26. Condenser Microphone- More delicate and sensitive microphone that requires electronic power supply

27. Large-diaphragm Condenser Mic- Specifically designed to pick-up lower frequencies in drums, human voice and other instruments with strong bass ranges; usually at least 1" diameter

28. Polar Pattern- (Mic Pattern)The area of pickup of a microphone based on a design that purposefully rejects sound from certain directions; allowing it to focus specifically on single sources and record a specific source while eliminating other undesirable sound.

29. Pick-up- a small microphone that is mounted on a musical instrument, usually permanently, and usually picks up the sound through direct vibrations of the instrument, and not through vibrations of the air, like a microphone.

30. Mic Stand- Holds the microphone in a secure, stationary position, often isolating it from mechanical contact with resonating surfaces

31. Mic Boom- an extension arm of a mic stand that allows overhead placement of a mic without interfering with movement of performers

32. Shock mount- Holds mic in mic stand and isolates it from resonating or original frequencies conducted through the stand; makes a quieter cleaner recording

33. Windscreen- a foam cover for the microphone that keeps moving air from interfering with the mic diaphragm without affecting sound transmission

34. Pop-filter- a thin piece of fabric placed in front of a microphone to reduce or eliminate plosive "p" air blasts that overload the mic diaphragm

35. Direct box- a pre-amplifier that allows line-level musical instruments such as guitars and keyboards to be connected to a mixing board and avoid playing through an amplifier.

36. Transducer- changes sound to electrical energy (microphone or pick-up) and electrical energy to sound (speakers, headphone)

Recording/Mixing/Processing/Playback

37. Mixer/Mixing Board/Console- Electronic console that allows for adjustment of many aspects of sound including volume, tone, effects, listening to, and routing of signals

38. Switch- electrical control that opens or closes a particular circuit allowing the signal access to that circuit; several types used in audio include rocker, push-button, slider, toggle, rotating, etc.

39. Gain/Trim- initial volume control on mixer channel strip; usually at pre-amp stage; usually a twist knob

40. Pad- decreases volume a single fixed amount (-10dB usually); usually a push-button switch on a mixer, or a toggle switch

41. Fader- slider knob that is main control for volume of a single mixing board channel or group

42. Attenuator-Controls the amount of loudness/amplitude, either as a fixed switch or variable control that can adjust from 100% blockage to 100% passage; variable can be rotating or linear slider

43. Compressor- Audio processor that automatically and gradually reduces volume through several adjustable parameters to keep the volume in a specific range thereby preventing clipping without distracting, un-natural artifacts

44. Limiter- Audio processor that sets an absolute specific volume above which no louder signal may pass.

45. Reverb- Indistinct multiple echoes that add richness, depth and authenticity to a recording

46. Equalizer-adjusts the volume of selected frequency bands "tone control"

47. Low Cut/High Pass Filter- Eliminates lower pitch frequencies like HVAC systems or building rumble

48. High Cut/Low Pass Filter – Eliminates higher pitch frequencies like various hiss and ringing

49. Roll-off Filter – Attenuates frequencies at the high or low end of the scale in a fixed ratio;

50. Hi, Mid, Low- the three most common divisions of frequency bands in an equalizer

51. Special Effect Processor- Electronic processors that allow extensive adjustment of volume, compression, EQ, and Reverb to modify the original signal (there are dozens of effects including chorus, notch filters, flanging, dynamic EQs)

52. Monitor- (as in Audio Monitor) loudspeakers or headphones used to listen to the signal to be recorded or played back

53. Mute- to silence a specific recording source at the mixing board; usually a push-button switch

54. Pan- shifts sound to left or right outputs (as in panorama)

55. Solo- plays one channel exclusively, while silencing all the others; good for adjusting one single source coming into the mixer

56. Pre-amp- (Pre-amplifier) the first stage of audio processors that electronically boosts an electric signal received from a microphone or electronic sound source (electric guitar) to make it more easily processed by other recording equipment like mixers.

57. Amplifier- boosts the volume level of an electronic signal through tubes, transistors, and integrated circuitry to a sufficient amount that will drive loudspeakers and headphones for listening to playback.

58. Signal to Noise Ratio (S/N)-range noting the number of dB between the noise floor and usable signal

59. Auxiliary Send-sends signal to external signal effects processor (black box); generally used to send a group of channels.

60. Auxiliary Return- feeds processed signal sent from "Aux Send" back into the mixer to blend with original signal

61. Insert- sends single channel to external signal processor (similar to Aux Send and Return), and returns the processed signal to the mixing panel

62. PFL- pre-fader listen- monitors input despite fader level (similar to solo;)
63. Peak meter- reads volume peaks only
64. VU meter – reads average audio volume
65. Output Select- button that routes the mixing board channel to a particular output (monitor, main out, recording channel (s)
66. Distortion/Clipping – Exceeding the ability of audio equipment/software to handle the volume level; accurate playback deteriorates to noise.
67. Ground hum- Electronic noise created by Alternating Current (AC) electrical waves that leak into the audio chain.
68. Proximity effect – the closer to the mic a sound occurs, the louder the bass level
69. Mastering- the final stage of mixing where levels are matched, songs assembled, and final EQ and compression may be applied.
70. Patch Bay – central switching point enabling different pieces of audio equipment to be connected to each other by easily accessible patch cables.
71. Recording chain- mic, record/mixer amplifier, processor, recorder, player, playback amplifier, loudspeaker
72. DAW- Digital Audio Workstation- a computer system with components specific to audio production such as a high-quality sound card with professional inputs for microphones and playback, quality monitoring equipment, a large visual display, and advanced audio recording/processing software applications
73. Baffle- In a recording studio, a sound-absorbing panel used to isolate sound sources (e.g. singer, drummer) thereby limiting unwanted leakage of sound into other microphones.
74. Balanced/Unbalanced- Balanced cables have a ground/shield conductor and are less susceptible to electronic interference. Unbalanced are generally non-professional, cheaper items.
75. Music Amplifier- a piece of equipment used to boost musical instrument sound during a public performance that includes inputs, power amplifier and loudspeakers; frequently have built in Effects Processors, EQ and various volume controls.
76. Click track/metronome- Computer-generated beats that play in a set rhythm used as a guide for performers to keep a set time; very helpful in multi-track recording when tracks are recorded at different times.

77. Over-dub- Recording individual music tracks at a different times that will be eventually mixed into a single recording

78. White noise - all frequencies played at once; resulting in a hissing sound; useful for testing equipment.

79. Pink Noise - all frequencies played at once, but with bass frequencies boosted.

80. Sample Rate- In digital audio, the rate at which analog sound is sampled in the digital recording process. In CDs it is a minimum of 44.1kHz/second, which is generally accepted as the rate at which no signal degradation occurs.

81. Control Room – Houses all the processing gear and monitor equipment separate from the recording space so monitoring will not interfere with recording; usually equipped with a window or video link and sound-lock doors into the recording studio.

Editing

82. Fade- reduction of audio level (amplitude) from normal to inaudible at varying speeds.

83. Room Tone- ambient sound recorded in a room that is background to the desired sound; includes people talking, HVAC, refrigerator motors, music from a radio, highway traffic, airplanes, and other noise; usually unwanted, but needed to create illusion of smooth audio editing

84. Cross Fade- two tracks of audio blending into each other by reducing one track to inaudible level while increasing the other to normal level

85. Timeline- visual representation of an audio recording illustrating the changes the audio makes as it progresses through time.

86. Track- one channel of recorded audio, recorded independently of others

87. Waveform- A view in the timeline that shows amplitude/volume changes in a region (not frequency)

88. Effects/Processors- electronically change the volume and timbre of an event/region through software

89. Cut-split an event/region

90. Zoom control- Zoom into track to more precisely edit specific wave forms or sections of the track

91. Selection- highlight a section of the time line to individually adjust that section with efx, volume, trimming and other changes without affecting other non-selected sections.
92. Pre-set- a collection of software settings that determine the parameters of an effect or switch to enable an exact replication of that effect.
93. Keyboard shortcuts- automatic selection of software commands by pressing a key or combination of 2-3 keys instead of mousing through multiple menu screens.
94. Group/Ungroup- combine several events or commands to move as a group; ungroup releases the group into individually move events
95. Master- a bus that controls all tracks with volume and/or effect changes
96. Bus- a routing of a track to an output or other channel or other controller
97. Tools- Methods of controlling editing activities the time line in distinct fashions (grabber, selector, trimmer, zoomer, etc)

Radio

98. Program- A broadcast segment, usually at least 30 minutes long, or up to 5 hours that features specific content like music, news, talk, or sports.
99. Spot- A commercial or non-commercial announcement that either sells or gives community information. Can be recorded or read live.
100. Bumper- A short segment or break between main show segments that can introduce the segment, ID the station, show, announcer, special segment; can be highly produced or just a sting.
101. Sting- 1-3 second sound effect or music bit that acts as a bumper, accent or commentary (often humorous).
102. Broadcast clock- A station's broadcast schedule as it follows the time of day.
103. Weight- the number of times a song is played during the broadcast clock; usually measuring its popularity
104. Call-in- A listener calls in during a program to speak on the air live with the announcer/host.

105. Request line-A phone line that records listener song requests for songs to be played on the air.
106. PSA- Public Service Announcement; a recorded spot giving information about a public or non-profit event or service.
107. EBS- Emergency Broadcast System; sends announcements warning of severe weather or other emergency situations to all broadcast stations which automatically switch from regular programming to transmit the short emergency announcement
108. Transmitter- feeds electrical broadcast signal to tower
109. AM/FM- Amplitude Modulation, Frequency Modulation; types of terrestrial electrical radio broadcasting
110. Streaming- Sending broadcast signal over the Internet to server that distributes multiple Internet feeds.
111. Automation- Plays music playlists from a radio station library and other pre-recorded material according to pre-programmed timeline without human operation
112. ASCAP/BMI- American Society of Composers, Artists and Publishers and Broadcast Music Incorporated collect royalties from broadcasters and other commercial entities and distribute those royalties to copyright holders of the intellectual properties.
113. ISDN-Integrated Services Digital Network- transmission network for high quality audio and video over copper land lines usually owned by a telephone company
114. MP3- popular highly compressed audio file used on small portable digital players like the i-pod or for sending across the Internet, where bandwidth is limited
115. Copy-Written material meant for broadcast including news bits, weather, promotion, commercial spot and more.
116. Tag- The beginning and/or end of a commercial spot for a national product that customizes it for a local area.
117. Backsell- DJ patter about a previous song
118. Frontsell-DJ patter about the next song.
119. Liner- Short bit of copy read by an announcer from a card, usually no music background
120. Donut- The middle part of a commercial spot for a national product that customizes it for a local area
121. Sweep- Pre-recorded highly produced ID for a radio station
122. Promo- A spot that promotes a program on a station
123. Dub- A copy of a commercial or program

124. DMCA- Digital Millennium Copyright Act- Federal laws that regulate the use of copyrighted material on the Internet so that royalties can be collected and paid to copyright holders.

125. Syndication- Programs transmitted by Internet or satellite that have been produced elsewhere. They require no local production staff. Stations pay a license fee for each broadcast.

126. Satellite Feed- Program originated in a distant production center that is sent by satellite to a station for live or recorded broadcast.

127. Automation- Playback of pre-recorded programs controlled by computer software that follows a pre-assembled playlist that plays programs and program segments at specific times of the day.

128. Music Library- All the songs immediately available to an announcer or producer; may be on CD or as digital files on hard-drives.

129. Playlist-The list of program materials assembled by a producer to create a complete program which includes components like music, news, commercial spots, backsell, etc.

Jobs in the Field of Audio

1. Assistant Audio Duties
   a. Set up mic stands
   b. Set and position mics
   c. Run cables
   d. Setup talent monitors
   e. Setup House monitors
   f. Setup crew communications
   g. Trouble shoot
   h. Locate electric power sources
   i. Assist mixer during performance
   j. Clean and wrap equipment
   k. Report problems to chief
   l. Clean up location following event

- Radio
  o On-air talent
  o Audio Producer (spots)
  o Board Operator

- TV
  o On-air talent
  o Live Audio engineer
  o Audio/Postproduction Editor
  o Assistant Audio

- Theater/Live
  o House engineer
  o FOH engineer Mixer
  o Assist Audio

- Road
  o Road engineer/mixer
  o Road Audio Asst.

- Recording Studio
  o Recording Engineer
  o Audio Mixer
  o Post-Production Editor
  o Sound EFX Engineer/Foley Artist
  o Voice Talent
  o Asst Audio
  o Composer

-     o Session Musician
-     o Audio Book recording and editing
- Venue- Club, Hospitality, Conference Center, Hotel Meeting, Hospital, Shopping Center, Government Center, Schools, Colleges, Corporate Training Center, Churches, Cruise ships, Resorts
  - o A/V Technician
  - o A/V Mixer
  - o Produce A/V spots
- Equipment
  - o Sales
  - o Rental
  - o Repair
  - o Home, business, car audio equipment Installation
- Gaming
  - o Audio Producer/
  - o Audio Programmer

- Party/Event Creative DJ
  - o Club/Hospitality
  - o Location
  - o Lighting/video helpful
- Location Event Sound Reinforcement Company
  - o Location scouting and bidding
  - o Set-up, Teardown
  - o Live mixing operation of radio mics, playback, audio feeds,
  - o Band mixing
  - o Assistant audio
- Forensic/Legal audio
  - o Recording court room proceedings
  - o Recording depositions on location
  - o Cleaning up evidence recordings (911 recordings, bugs, accidental recordings
- Educational institutions
  - o Community education groups (YMCA, Art Centers, Government seminars, churches)
  - o Private technical schools
  - o High School, College
- Cable TV/Alarm system installation and maintenance

Tips for creating a recorded music playlist

The object of a music play list is to entertain an audience with an appealing selection of music played in an appealing sequence. It can also involve "DJ patter" which introduces a song, comments on it, or gives an interesting factoid, and enhances the musical performance. Many live music performers pepper their shows with comments about the works they perform; which makes an appealing program.

Ways to transition from one piece to another:
- Fade-out, silence,Fade- in
    - Many songs do this naturally.
    - If song is too long, operator can create the fades.
- Dissolve/mix
    - As one song fades out, another fades in on top of it
- Blank space
    - This is a short segment of silence between songs; as in an album
- Voice over
    - The DJ talks over the beginning or end of the song with an introduction, or finishing another piece of business like news, commercial, phone call, etc.
- Voice solo
    - The DJ speaks during the blank spot between music with "DJ patter"
- Sweeper
    - A pre-recorded just a few seconds long break that IDs the station, the program/DJ, or the station "brand;" like "more music per hour on Lite 102"

Considerations for an appealing playlist:
- Variety
    - Not all songs sound the same; different pace, instruments, transitions, lengths, etc. are used
    - Sometimes it's good to be similar, sometimes dissimilar
    - There's no exact prescription for a good playlist. You learn by listening to others.
- Consistent theme/style
    - Hard rock, classical, jazz, rap, folk, new age, country, oldies rock, Americana, R&B
- Is the list entertaining or irritating due to mismatch or chaos?

- Beat: Do songs have similar rhythms?
- Key: Are songs in the same key?
- Instrumentation: Do songs have the same instruments?
- Performer: Are songs by the same or similar performers?
- Vocal: Are songs primarily vocal or instrumental?
- Audience: Does the audience like the musical style?

Common Radio Program Components

1. Recorded Music
2. Audience call-ins
3. Live Music
4. Recorded PSA
5. Liner- Read Announcement/PSA
6. Legal Station ID
7. Weather Report
8. Traffic Report
9. In-studio Interview
10. In-Studio Panel Discussion/Interview
11. Opinion/Editorial/Com-mentary
12. Local/National/Inter-national News
13. Concert Calendar
14. Station Promo- General information about the station, encouraging people to tune in
15. Program Promo - General information about a program, encouraging people to tune in
16. Program ID (Drop)- short ("You're listening to Sports Talk on WSGE, and I'm Dave Hodges)
17. Promo (The best webcast in the Southeast—Studio 321 Internet Radio)
18. Back Sell (Song info following the song)
19. Front Sell (Song info preceding the song)
20. Bumper Music ("It's Raining Men" leading into live weather report)
21. Stinger (Sound Effect- "Boiiiinggg")
22. Music News – current event
23. Music Trivia – interesting factoid
24. Color Commentary – extended comment about music just played or about to be played

Tips for Quality Radio/Audio Spot Production

1. Use Compression
2. Use EQ
3. Use fade-ins and fade-outs
4. Name tracks in your multi-track window
5. Name, project number in audio files names
6. Produce in multi-track and save all tracks in .ses
7. Structure music to have a beginning, middle and end in program parts
8. Have music lead the voice
9. Duck music when voice enters and leaves
10. At the end, fade music out after the voice finishes, except if music has a natural end.
11. Make effects relevant to subject
12. Make voice the primary part
13. Make the voice clear

Recording Studio Preparation and Procedure Checklist

Allow 60-90 minutes to prepare for a recording session, prior to performers' arrival. Be sure you have contacted the performers before the session to confirm their arrival, title of work to be recorded, and instruments expected at session.

1. Connect all sets of headphones to proper headphone amp
2. Set all mics in convenient locations; check their operation, including compressor inserts
3. Turn on racks and start software
4. Create performer folder on desktop and project folder in it
5. Create a session in the software. Make a test record and playback
6. Name tracks with expected instruments
7. Keep written session notes; include names of performers and instruments
8. Turn off all cell phones
9. Offer performers, especially singers, a mug of water
10. Leave 3-4 seconds blank at head and tail on every recording
11. Immediately save session at end of every take—**save all associated files**
12. Clean-up studio and put all gear in proper storage.

Recording Studio Engineer Qualification Test

Engineer-in-Charge must pass an evaluation consisting of preparing Control A for session, connecting **3 mics and 1 direct box** in the studio, setting up a Pro Tools session with **3 tracks**.

1. Set stands, mics, mic accessories.
2. Connect mics via cables to Studio Panel.
3. Connect and place Furman headphone mixers.
4. Turn on all Control-A equipment racks in proper sequence.
5. Turn on computer.
6. Turn on loudspeakers in Control A.
7. Create appropriate session folders in appropriate drives.
8. Create a Pro Tools session with 3 tracks and 3 monitor channels.
9. Create or use existing **performer folder** on **Internal Media Hard Drive**; create a **project** sub-folder in it.
10. Create a new sub-folder **for each song**; each song should have its own session, but additional takes of the same song should be in the same session time line.
11. **Start Protools.**
12. Set up a new session named with the song title.
13. Save session in pre-named folder (step #10).
14. Use 44.1 khz /24 bit session setting.
15. Create and name tracks with expected instruments.
16. Put mic names in comment headers.
17. Create a Stereo Master Track.
18. Set proper inputs, outputs and monitor sends in Pro Tools using "gastonnormal01" pre-set.
19. Check mic operation/continuity in pre-amps.
20. Set up 4-channel performer headphone mix in ProTools Send section.
21. Check that all Furman studio headphone monitors are working with proper gain levels.
22. Test record and playback of all expected mics, speakers, and headphone monitoring.
23. Set proper record levels at all in/out gain stages (be sure phantom is on).
24. Back up the Session on the Seagate 1 external drive.

Common Cable/Adapter/Connector Chart

	RCA to RCA Cable Stereo M-F		BNC (data and video) Connector Mono M-Solder
	RCA to RCA Cable Mono M-M		XLR to RCA Adapter Mono F-F
	XLR to XLR Cable Mono M-F		XLR to ¼"TRS Adapter Mono M-F
	¼"TRS to TRS Cable Stereo M-M		XLR to ¼"TRS Adapter Mono M-M
	Mini-phone TRS Cable Stereo M-M		XLR to Mini-phone Adapter Mono M-F
	TRS to TRS Cable Mono M-M (Guitar Cable)		XLR to XLR Adapter-Coupler Mono F-F
	XLR Connector Mono M		RCA to RCA Adapter-Coupler Mono FF
	XLR Connector Mono F		RCA to Mini-phone Adapter Stereo F-M
	¼"TRS Connector Mono or Stereo F		¼" TRS to Mini-Phone Adapter Stereo M-F (Headphone)
	¼"TRS Connector Stereo M		RCA-RCA Adapter Cable Mono Splitter 1M-2F
	Tiny Telephone TRS Connector Stereo M-Solder-Patch Panel		¼" TRS to Mini-phone Adapter Cable Stereo to Mono L+R M-M

	RCA to Mini Phone Adapter Cable Stereo M-M			¼"TRS to Mini-phone Adapter Cable Stereo to Stereo M-M
	¼"TRS to XLR Adapter Cable Stereo to Mono M-F			RCA to Mini-phone Adapter Cable Stereo to Stereo M-F
	16 ch. Cable Snake XLR+TRS Mono XLRM-XLRF			

Also by Robert Maier

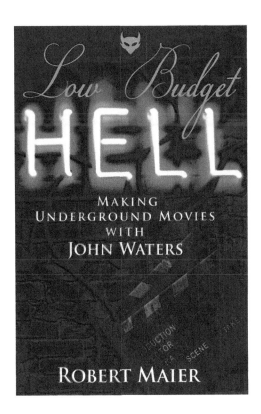

 "Outrageous dirt"- John Waters
"A great time" – *Indiewire.com*
"A fascinating tale – *Videoscope Magazine*
"An invaluable collection of juicy stories that will please
Waters devotees and fans of underground cinema" –
Montreal Mirror
"Dishy" – *The Advocate*

Available from Amazon.com and booksellers worldwide.

New York – Oslo - Charlotte

NOTES:

NOTES:

NOTES:

CPSIA information can be obtained at www.ICGtesting.com
Printed in the USA
BVOW10s0657090814

362250BV00001B/1/P